Drawing and Sketching

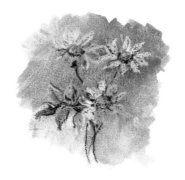

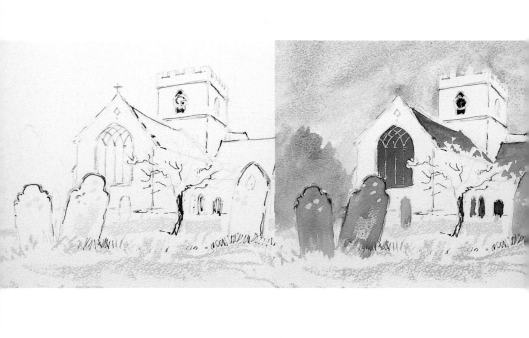

Drawing and Sketching

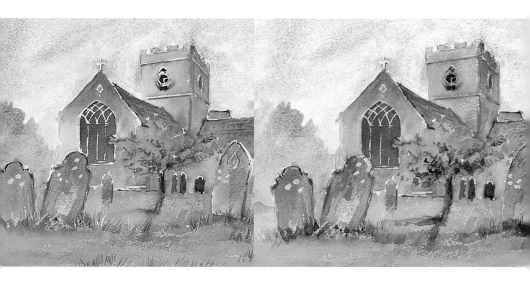

Jackie Simmonds ● **Wendy Jelbert** ● **Marie Blake**

ISBN-10: 0-00-719327-0
ISBN-13: 978-0-00-719327-1

ISBN-10: 0-06-081886-7 (in the United States)
ISBN-13: 978-0-06-081886-9

FIRST U.S. EDITION
HarperCollins books may be purchased for educational, business, or sales promotional use. For information in the United States, please write to: Special Markets Department, HarperCollins Publishers, 10 East 53rd Street, New York, NY 10022.

The name of the "Smithsonian," "Smithsonian Institution," and the sunburst logo are registered trademarks of the Smithsonian Institution.

All illustrations © Jackie Simmonds 2005 except for the following:
Marie Blake: pages 24, 25, 34, 40, 41, 42, 43, 44, 45, 58, 59, 79, 89, 90, 91, 92, 94, 105, 120, and 121
Wendy Jelbert pages 2, 3, 26, 29, 31, 32, 34, 48, 50, 51, 52, 57, 60, 61, 63, 66, 67, 69, 71, 78, 84, 88, 91, 93, 95, 96, 97, 100, 102, 106, 109, 110, 111, 113, 162, 168, 169, 170, 171, 174, 175, 176, 180, 181, 186, and 187

Marie Blake, Wendy Jelbert, and Jackie Simmonds assert the moral right to be identified as the authors of this work.

Printed and bound by Printing Express Ltd. Hong Kong

10 09 08 07 06 05
9 8 7 6 5 4 3 2 1

contents

The authors   6

Introduction   8

materials and techniques   12

composing a picture   34

fruits and vegetables   52

natural forms   72

plants and flowers   84

trees   100

skies   114

water   126

landscapes   136

people and animals   150

buildings   162

seaside   176

Need to know more?   188

Index   190

The authors

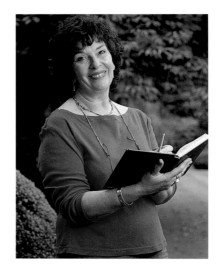

Jackie Simmonds

Jackie Simmonds began to paint in her thirties, attending art school as a full-time "mature student". She is now a busy painter and art instruction author. Her work is exhibited in both mixed exhibitions and one-woman shows, and reproductions of her work have been distributed worldwide. Jackie writes articles for *The Artist* magazine, runs workshops and painting vacations, and has written five art instruction books and made six painting videos.

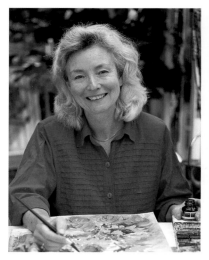

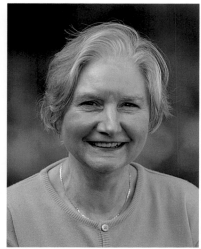

Wendy Jelbert

Wendy Jelbert has painted from a young age, and her three children and grandchildren do the same! She attended art school, studying fine and abstract art, pottery, and printmaking. She exhibits in England at the Century Gallery in Hartley Wintney, Hampshire, First Floor Gallery in Romsey, Hampshire, Burford Gallery in Burford, Oxfordshire, and Wykenham Gallery in Stockbridge, Hampshire. She runs workshops and has made 5 art instruction videos and written 14 books.

Marie Blake

Marie Blake trained as a painter at Kingston-upon-Thames School of Art, England, and later qualified as a teacher of art at Central College, London University, London, England. She has taught art at both primary and high school level and also has extensive experience of teaching leisure painters. Marie exhibits her own paintings, and she is a regular contributor to *Leisure Painter* magazine. Her first book *You Can Paint Pastels* was published by HarperCollins Publishers.

Introduction

As a child, you probably loved spending time being creative. Even tiny toddlers love to grab a pencil or crayon and will scribble away with intense pleasure. Of course, children are completely uninhibited and, in their innocence, will be delighted with the results that they achieve, whatever these look like. As adults, our inhibitions grow, and we often are embarrassed if we produce less than perfect results, especially when we are encouraged to show our efforts to others. This book will encourage you to give drawing and sketching a try, regardless of any lack of experience, in order to rediscover the pure joy to be gained from them.

Learning to sketch is great fun, and although the word "learning" implies a duty, it is important to remember that learning can be very exciting, challenging, and, most importantly, rewarding. Your confidence will grow, and tentative beginnings will soon develop into positive results. Best of all, you don't need to be an expert draftsperson to enjoy sketching—absolute accuracy is not essential for most sketches, and often it is the unfinished quality of a sketch that adds to its appeal.

When you make a sketch, you are not necessarily producing a work that will end up on the walls of an art gallery. Sketches can be made for a variety of reasons: to collect information, to explore

▼ You don't have to use a pencil, pen, or charcoal for sketching. These sheep were sketched with watersoluble art pens.

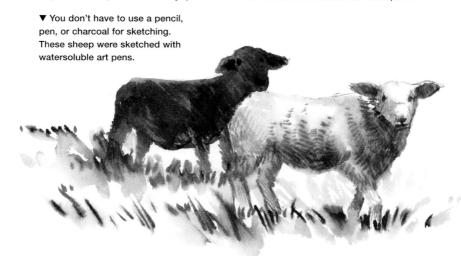

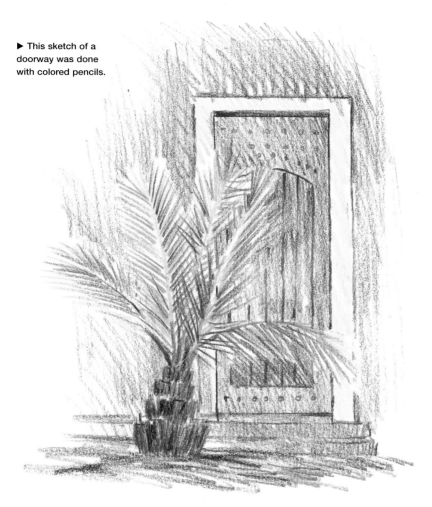

▶ This sketch of a doorway was done with colored pencils.

possible subjects for later pictures, or even just for fun. What matters is that with every sketch you make, you learn something about drawing and also improve your eye/hand coordination skills and your powers of observation. This will help you establish a firm foundation from which you will be able to grow as a creative individual.

Look at this book as a valuable source of help and information, while you practice and develop your sketching language. You can keep your sketchbooks completely private—after all, they should be working exercise books. Nurture your budding talent gently, and only when you feel ready do you need to show others the results of your efforts. That may be sooner than you think, as long as you work with a positive attitude and practice, practice, practice!

How to use this book

This is an art instruction book for beginners, containing a wide variety of examples, exercises, and demonstrations. However, what it does not contain is reams of text. Although some written, or verbal, explanation is obviously very useful, there is still nothing like the physical act of making a sketch yourself or watching a teacher.

Every page of this book offers you an example of a sketch, and each exercise is simply and clearly explained and broken down into simple steps that are easy for you to follow. By all means, copy the examples given, but once you have tried out an exercise, and become familiar with the techniques explained, the best course of action is to find a similar object, or subject, and then to work from life, using the basic principles and techniques that you have been shown.

You will notice that we have not always been specific about the "names" of the colors that have been used. This is because there are many different manufacturers of art materials on the market, and each manufacturer uses slightly different names. Don't worry about this; simply use a color that is similar to the one shown; that will be fine.

The exercises and examples are generally relatively short and straightforward. However, in some of the chapters you will find a slightly longer demonstration piece, that is broken down into several more steps for you to follow.

Throughout the book, a variety of sketching tools has been used to

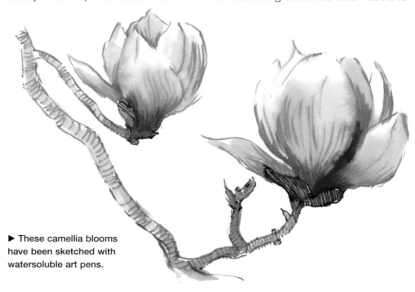

▶ These camellia blooms have been sketched with watersoluble art pens.

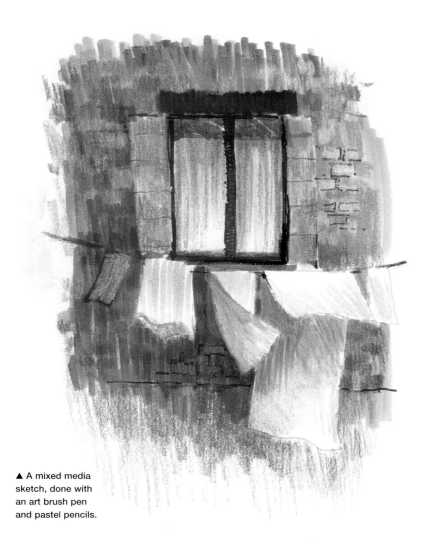

▲ A mixed media
sketch, done with
an art brush pen
and pastel pencils.

enable you to become familiar with
different materials, including lead
pencils, colored and conté pencils,
watersoluble colored pencils, art
brush pens, charcoal, pastels, inks,
and even watercolors. You may
like some materials, and some
subjects better than others; it is
important to discover what you like
to draw and the materials you enjoy
using. Keep an open mind and be
prepared to try everything.

As you practice, your own style
will gradually emerge. Always work
in a sketchbook, and by the time
you have filled it, you will find that
your drawing fluency and skills will
have improved significantly.

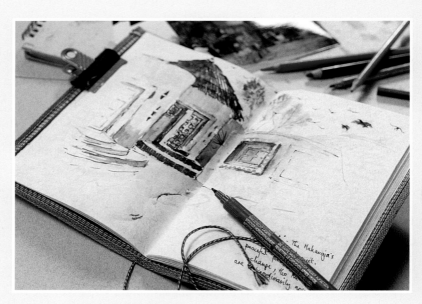

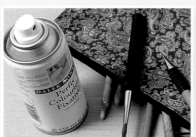

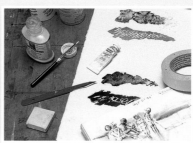

techniques

You cannot start drawing and sketching, without learning about your materials and the kinds of marks you can make with them. It is essential to practice and have fun at the same time. Enjoy every moment, throw yourself into learning with enthusiasm and an open mind, and soon you will be on your way to producing great drawings and sketches.

Basic materials

You will find all kinds of different drawing media in your art materials store, and although no one drawing medium is superior to any other, some are more popular than others— especially lead pencils, charcoal, and conté sticks, which have proved their versatility over the years. It is only by trial and error—or perhaps trial and success—that you will discover which medium suits you the best.

A range of drawing and sketching materials are used throughout this book, some of which are traditional, whereas others are more modern. There are many innovative materials that are now available, such as watersoluble pencils and art brush pens, which have a firm point at one end, just like a fiber-tip pen, and a softer, brushlike tip at the other end.

In addition, you can have fun experimenting with pastels, conté, colored inks, watercolors, and other media. The selection is varied enough for you to enjoy discovering a fascinating range of drawing and sketching possibilities.

▼ Sketching materials can be simple and very lightweight. For the basics, all you need is a sketchbook and some pencils.

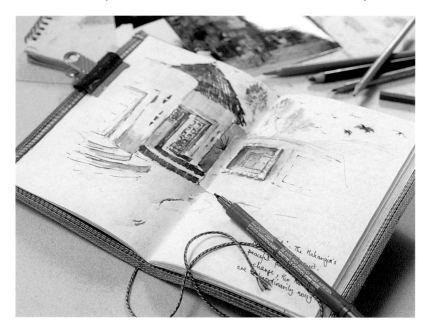

Suggested materials

Some popular drawing materials are:

- **Lead pencils** Start with grades HB (medium hard), 2B (soft), and 4B (very soft). Always buy good quality (more expensive) pencils, since the better quality pencils have the lead bonded to the wooden casing to prevent the lead from breaking if you drop them. It is very frustrating to try to sharpen a pencil only to discover that the lead is broken all the way down to the bottom. Ask for advice at your local art materials store if you are not sure which manufacturer's products to choose.

- **Charcoal sticks** These are available in various sizes. It is probably best to buy a mixed box.

- **Charcoal pencils (compressed charcoal)** This is useful for more detailed work.

- **Conté** This is available in both stick and pencil form.

- **Pastel pencils** These are thin sticks of hard pastel in pencil form.

- **Colored pencils** These are clean and portable.

- **Watersoluble colored pencils** The marks can be dissolved to give a watercolor wash effect.

- **Art brush pens** These are pens with a fine tip at one end and a brush at the other.

▶ Here are some of the sketching implements used in this book, listed above, next to the marks that they make.

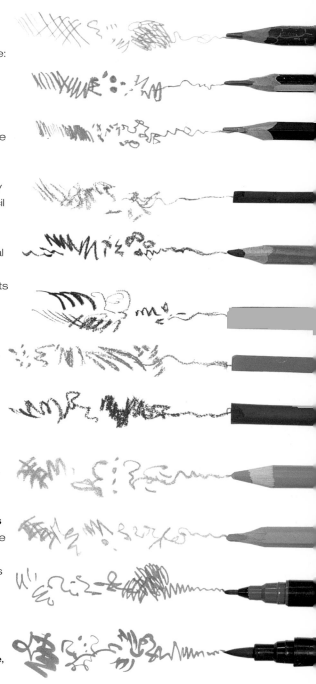

Other materials

In addition to the basic materials already mentioned, you may want to expand your range and try other media, such as those listed below.

Pastels

You will need traditional pastels and oil pastels. You can buy a set of one-inch (2.5-cm) long soft pastels. Round pastels create soft effects, whereas the square, firmer ones are good for fine details. Your set of oil pastels should contain the "fatter" varieties, as these are better at resisting watercolors (they repel watercolor paint and let the pastel color show through) than the harder, smaller varieties. These can also be bought separately. Include some lighter colors, such as pale cream, grays, greens, pinks, and white.

Drawing pens

These include felt-tip and fiber-tip pens, available separately or in sets. The "throw-away" drawing pens with steel nibs are excellent, especially a black and sepia in sizes 01 and 02 in both waterproof and watersoluble inks. There is also an excellent pen for sketching that needs cartridges; it is slightly more expensive but worth the extra. Again, use both black and sepia.

Colored inks

It is a good idea to purchase a set of colored inks in pots: choose your favorite colors to try out. They can be applied with a dipper, a ruling/drawing pen, or a brush.

▼ Watercolors are a great medium for making sketches. All you need is different colored paints in tubes and trays, some brushes, and special watercolor paper.

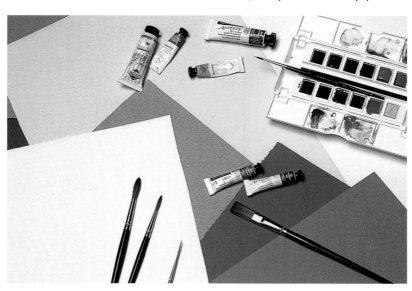

Some watercolor paints are very transparent; others are more opaque. Make a note in your sketchbook the properties of various colors; they can affect the quality of your washes.

Watercolors

Two qualities of watercolor paints are available: Students' and Artists'. They come in both trays and tubes. We suggest that you buy a tray set of watercolors in Artists' quality. You can always add more colors later on as you need them.

Just before you start working, always wet the dry surface of your trays to prime them for painting. You will need to include the primary colors—red, blue, and yellow—from which all the other colors can be mixed. We suggest that you also buy Yellow Ocher, Burnt Sienna, Cerulean Blue, and a ready-mixed green (Hooker's or Olive Green), plus a dark brown.

White gouache

This thick "covering" white paint is supplied in tubes; it may be used on its own or mixed with watercolors. It is also useful for making alterations and correcting mistakes.

Brushes

Although sable brushes are the best you can buy, the synthetic ones or sable/synthetic mix are ideal. You will need a selection of brushes: a no. 5

and no. 10 round-headed, a no. 12 flat-headed, and also a rigger no. 1. Remember, the higher the number, the larger the brush.

You will also need

● **An eraser** A putty eraser is best for charcoal, and a firmer, plastic eraser for pencil.

● **A craft knife** This is useful for sharpening your pencils.

● **Fixative** This is a spray used to prevent drawings from smudging.

● **Masking fluid** This is good when working with watercolors for blotting out areas you don't want to paint. You also need an applicator.

● **A plastic palette** This is useful for preparing watercolor washes.

● **Bulldog clips** These are useful outdoors in windy weather, to keep your sketchbook open.

● **A sturdy pencil case** Or use a hinged, metal glasses case.

● **Drawing board** This is useful to attach your paper to. Masking tape could be used for this purpose.

● **A torchon** A rolled paper stump, for blending charcoal or conté.

● **A fine sandpaper block** This is used to create a sharp point on a pencil or a piece of charcoal.

● **A sketching easel** This is useful if you prefer not to work with your sketchbook on your knee.

● **A lightweight sketching stool** This is very useful outdoors.

● **A long stick for measuring** A small plant stake is ideal.

● **A bag** For all your equipment.

Sketchbooks

The variety of sketchbooks on the market can be bewildering. However, it's a good idea to have a selection of sketchbooks in different sizes, ranging from pocket-size to large. It is also interesting to try different surfaces. You will quickly discover that sketches on drawing paper, which is smooth, look very different from sketches on watercolor paper, which is often textured. A sketchbook with colored paper pages makes an interesting and challenging change from white paper.

Make sure that your sketchbooks have good, solid covers that will stand up to normal wear and tear. Also, if you plan to use watersoluble implements, it is sensible to use heavier papers—either a thick cartridge paper or a watercolor paper (see page opposite)—since thin, lightweight papers will buckle when you add any water. A spiral-bound sketchbook can be useful—if you like to work on one page, you can turn the rest back. If the book has a firm binding, do not be afraid to work across the center if you want to create a large drawing.

▼ You may need a selection of different sketchbooks, as illustrated here.

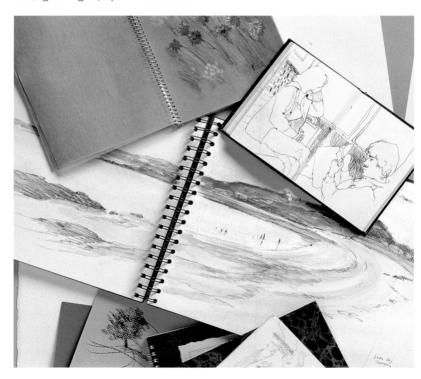

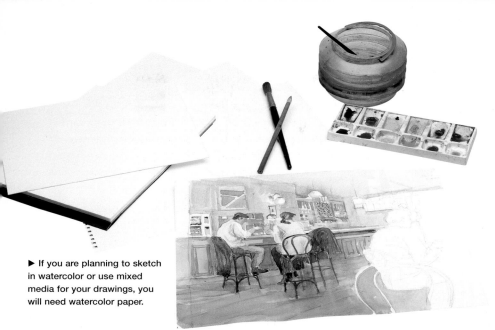

▶ If you are planning to sketch in watercolor or use mixed media for your drawings, you will need watercolor paper.

Paper

The specially-made watercolor papers are best for sketching in watercolor and mixed media. Their surface texture holds the liquid color and helps create a unique watercolor effect. You can use either Rough, Hot Press, or Cold Press paper. Cold Press is the one that is most commonly used by beginners. Paper weights vary but a 140 lb (300 gsm) watercolor paper, which is available in sheets, spiral-bound pads, or blocks, is ideal when you are starting out in watercolor sketching. If there is little watercolor used in your work, you can get away with a 190 lb (90 gsm) Not surface paper or pad.

You may also have fun working with colored papers. Heavyweight mount boards, scrapbook paper, or assorted colored paper pads for the brighter colors are ideal. Some pastel papers would also be fine. These have a textured surface to hold the pastel particles and are available in a wide range of colors. White paper can be used for studies, but mid-toned colored papers are the easiest for painting. A useful size is 9 x 12 inch (229 x 305 mm).

MUST KNOW

Using spray fixative

If your sketchbook does not contain tissue inserts between the pages, when working with pastels, conté, charcoal, or chalk pastel, give a finished sketch a burst of spray fixative to prevent it from transferring onto the opposite page.

Making marks

One of the best ways to learn about your materials is to analyze what they can do by making marks. Start off by producing some practice sheets, beginning with the most familiar of objects, the lead pencil. Don't expect your results to be identical to the ones that are illustrated here; everyone has their own personal handwriting.

Graphite lead pencils

Lead pencils are graded—those with an "H" designation are harder than those with a "B"—and thus 2B is soft, 6B is even softer; 2H is hard, and 6H is very hard. The softer the pencil, the blacker the mark it makes. Try using some HB, 2B, and 4B pencils and study the different effects.

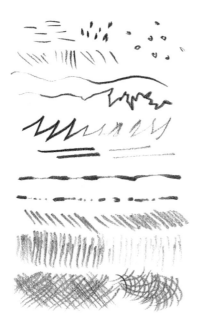

▲ To create an area of interesting texture, scribble with the point of a pencil, then use an eraser to soften lines and remove areas.

▲ Using the pencil point, try creating lots of lines. Vary the pressure on your pencil and make sure that you always keep the point long and sharp. Develop some parallel lines into areas of shading to create "tone." Then crisscross some lines in different directions; this is called "crosshatching."

▲ Sharpen the pencil to a long point and create an area of "tone" by using it on its side. Hold the pencil cupped in the palm of your hand, with your fingers pointing downward and the back of your hand facing upward. Add more graphite to the base of the shape as you work.

Charcoal

Charcoal is wonderfully versatile and easy to correct, so it is the perfect sketching medium for beginners. In stick form, it is especially good when it is used in a loose, sketching way that doesn't involve too much detail, and compressed charcoal sticks can be sharpened for detailed work. Charcoal work needs a spray of fixative to stop it from smudging.

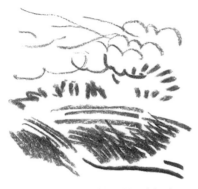

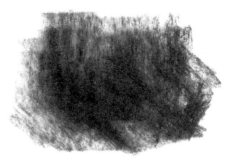

▲ Make some lines with a thin stick of charcoal, and then try some crosshatching, too. If you turn the stick in your fingers as you work, you can maintain a point. Then try this again with a charcoal pencil, just to see how different it feels.

▲ Use the side of a stick pressed against the paper to cover an area of paper—you will find that thicker sticks are easier to hold. Try using different types of paper to see the effects—watercolor paper breaks up the marks much more than smooth paper.

▲ Scribble some lines with the point of the charcoal and then blend, or smudge, them with a finger. This is a useful technique to master for creating lovely soft effects, with no hard edges or texture.

▲ Use charcoal on its side for a dense area of tone, and then lift out light areas with a piece of putty eraser. If you squeeze the putty eraser into a point, you can also lift out fine lines.

Conté

Conté, either in stick or pencil form, behaves like charcoal, but it is a lot harder. Nevertheless, it is still possible to blend colors by rubbing with a finger or a rolled paper stump (called a "torchon"). Conté is less "sooty" than charcoal, and colors can be mixed by laying one color on top of another. Conté comes in a variety of colors; try experimenting with the traditional black, white, and earth colors—sepia (dark brown), sanguine (terra-cotta) and bister (brown). In stick form, it can be sharpened to a point or used on its side for blocking in larger areas.

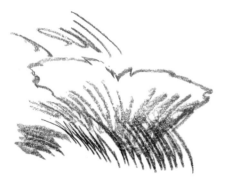

▲ Use one of the brown earth tones, together with a black conté stick or pencil, to try out linear marks. Work freely and swiftly.

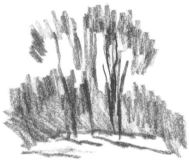

▲ Now try sanguine, which is a lovely, warm red. Vary the pressure as you work—your marks will be darker where you press harder.

▲ Break a small piece from a stick of conté and use it on its side, twisting your wrist as you work. The texture that you achieve will depend on the paper that you are using, so it may differ from the one shown above.

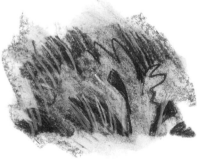

▲ Use the conté on its side, then smudge it with a finger. Scribble on top with a darker tone, and then try some white lines over the top. If you spray it with fixative before using white, the lines may be clearer.

Pastel pencils

Pastel pencils are essentially thin sticks of hard pastel in pencil form. Unlike ordinary sticks of pastel, the pencils are clean to use, and they will not break or crumble. They are excellent for color sketches, but they will need a spray of fixative to prevent them from smudging. You can use them in white sketchbooks, but it's also fun to try them on colored paper, so that you can use a white pencil in addition to colored ones.

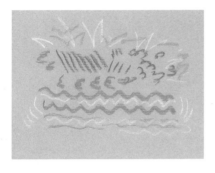

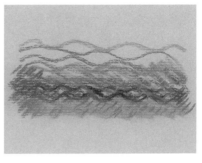

▲ Using colors of your own choice, make a variety of lines, dots, and stabbing marks, being conscious of the pressure you use and the effect you produce as a result.

▲ Now lay lines over each other to create a denser, more textured effect. Build up the area gradually, leaving some paper showing between the strokes.

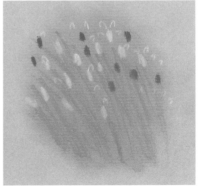

▲ Using three different colors, make three strips of lines, and then lightly blend with a finger. Blending will create a soft, diffused effect, a lot like a watercolor "wash."

▲ Blend two or three different blues together, and then make some lines over the top. Finally, finish off with white and blue dots, or any marks that appeal to you.

Pastels

You can be really inventive with a stick of pastel in your hand. The most important thing to realize is that the stick has a tip, but it also has a side surface—and you can, and should, use both. Also, you need to practice varying the pressure of your marks, since the kind of mark you make will vary dramatically, depending on the pressure that you use.

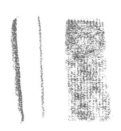 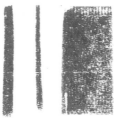  

▲ Make a light stroke (left); break the pastel and use its sharp edge for a thin line (center); drag a wide band with its full length (right).

▲ Repeat the process, but this time use increased pressure on the pastel. Notice the different effects that can be created.

▲ Working horizontally across the paper, graduate each stroke, progressing from heavy to light. Observe the different effect.

▲ Apply diagonal stripes: "close-hatching" or "infill."

▲ Repeat and blend by rubbing gently with tissue.

▲ Repeat and blend this time with a finger.

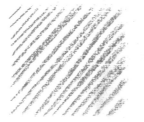  

▲ Make diagonal, spaced blue lines ("hatching").

▲ "Crosshatch" in a counter direction with yellow.

▲ Finger blend the yellow into the blue.

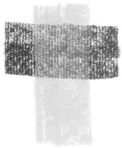

▲ Drag a band of blue next to a band of yellow, and then finger blend the two bands together.

▲ Drag a blue horizontal band, then cross it with a vertical yellow band. Notice the color blend.

▲ Repeat, but spray with some fixative before you apply the yellow. Notice the color separation.

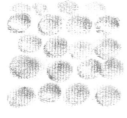

▲ Heavily infill blue, then finger blend gently, obscuring the individual strokes.

▲ Transfer the color that is left on your finger to make a fingerprint texture.

▲ Alternatively, rub the color into the paper to give a diffused texture.

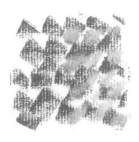

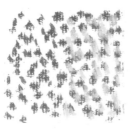

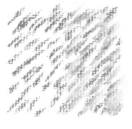

▲ Make blunt stipple marks with a short length of blue pastel; overlay with yellow.

▲ Make some sharp stipple marks in blue, and then repeat in yellow.

▲ Gently flick feathering strokes in blue, followed by some in yellow.

Traditional pastels on colored paper

Colored paper offers an exciting surface for pastels. You will need three different colored pastels for these examples.

a) Gently apply feathering strokes in one color and smudge it, follow it with a second color and smudge this, leaving some areas untouched, and add some strokes of the third color.

b) Wiggle a series of colors overlapping each other. Build up the area, leaving some paper showing between the shapes.

c) With definite sideways strokes apply a series of contrasting thick and thin hard-edged markings.

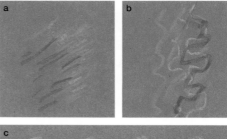

Oil pastels

These pastels will feel different than traditional pastels, but initially their markings are similar. The examples below are worked up using some colored paper and three different colored pastels.

a) Combine colored, blended areas over and under feathering strokes.

b) Make lines and dots using different parts of the pastel.

c) Scribble areas of different colors and then gently blend some of the color together, creating an effect similar to a watercolor wash.

d) Use different pressures to create a graded effect.

e) Try out sweeping movements with curling strokes, applying different pressures.

f) Crosshatch one color over another, and blend some of the pattern with a finger.

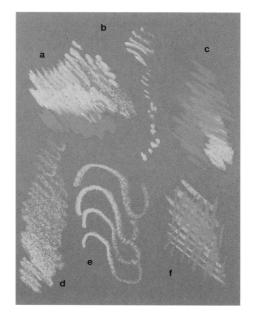

Colored wax pencils

Colored wax pencils will probably feel familiar to you—we all used them when we were children. They are clean and portable and available in a wide range of colors. They allow you to create areas of delicate color, as well as fine detail. Always sharpen your pencils to a long point, and as you work, practice rotating the pencil in your fingers to keep the point nice and sharp. Rather than pressing hard to achieve dense layers of color, which can make the surface slick and greasy, it is generally better to gently build up layers, allowing the white paper to "illuminate" the layers.

▲ Using one pencil, gradually build up the color, with a series of layers, thereby creating an area of tone.

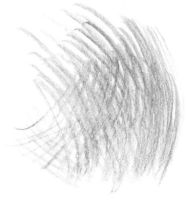

▲ Try two different colors and see how they create the illusion of a third color where they mix together.

▲ Now try two or three colors from the same "family" of colors: oranges, perhaps. Leave gaps of white paper to add sparkle. Areas of color created by using several similar colors have a lively, exciting feel.

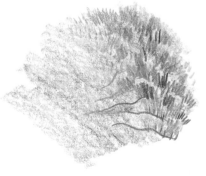

▲ Sharpen a pencil to a long point and, holding the pencil at its far end, scribble an area of color—the purple was used first here. Then try adding fine detail in many colors over the top.

Watersoluble colored pencils

These are a wonderful modern medium, that extend the versatility of colored pencils dramatically. Marks can be dissolved with a brush, sponge, or even a wet finger, to create fascinating watercolor wash effects. Then, when the paper is dry again, you can add more marks and areas of color. It is best to use watercolor paper or heavy drawing paper. Do not dip the pencil into water: dampen the tip with the end of a wet brush for softer marks.

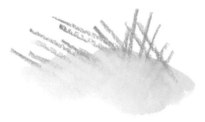

▲ Make simple lines, and then dissolve them into a puddle of water.

▲ Shade two colors together. Dissolve with water to see how a third color is created.

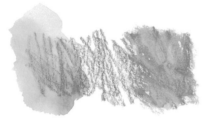

▲ Scribble an area of color. On the left-hand side, drop down a very wet puddle; on the right-hand side, use an almost dry brush to loosen the color. See how they differ.

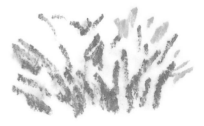

▲ Wet the paper first, and while it is still wet, make some marks and see how they soften and dissolve slightly.

▲ Make some lines, and then dab them with a wet sponge. Also, you can try scribbling directly onto the sponge with the long point of a pencil, and then you can make textural marks with your sponge—this technique is great for foliage.

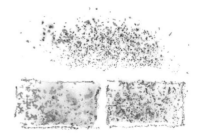

▲ Wet the paper and drop tiny pencil shavings cut with your craft knife down into the wet area. Firmer shavings will look like little curls of color. These "bricks" were drawn with a pencil, wet, then color was shaved into them for a textured effect.

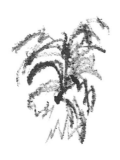  

▲ Dampen a pencil with water and twist it so that the pigment is applied both wet and dry onto the paper.

▲ Draw simple lines of color, trying out one, two, and three color crosshatching. Partially wet these, using a brush, then use the wash on the paper.

▲ Wet some of the paper and then pat the end of a brush over a wet pencil to splatter the colors. Note the different effect in the wet and dry areas.

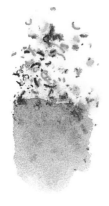 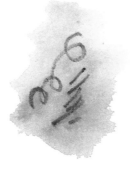 

▲ Wet the paper surface and scrape in splinterings with a knife, then wash over. Repeat to intensify the tone.

▲ Dampen a pencil with water and add a scribble to the paper. Wash over it; the pencil becomes indelible.

▲ Gradually build up the color using a series of feathered layers. Use a brush to wash over half.

▲ The darkest mark that can be obtained from a pencil is by placing a wet pencil tip on wet paper. When it is dry, apply a pale pencil, such as cream or white, to give a glazed area of light.

▲ Hold several wet colored pencil points together and blend them on a brush (like a palette), then transfer them onto a wet surface to diffuse together.

Pens

Fiber-tip, felt-tip, and marker pens are available in a wide variety of types and colors—try various types to see which ones you prefer. For these illustrations, watersoluble art pens have been used. They have a fine, firm point at one end and a useful, flexible brush tip at the other end. You can buy similar, waterproof ones, which are spirit- or alcohol-based. These are perhaps slightly better for overlaying colors, but they do have a tendency to "bleed through" the pages of drawing paper sketchbooks.

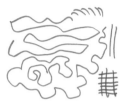

▲ The firm point of an art pen is excellent for lively drawing, but there is little variety in the line.

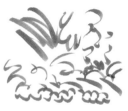

▲ Use the brush tip swiftly and freely, occasionally pressing firmly and then reducing the pressure to produce finer lines.

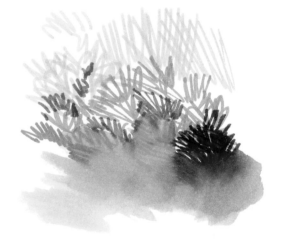

▲ Try different colors and shades together and use scribble and crosshatching. Float a little water over the bottom and see the ink dissolve into a soft wash.

▲ Using the brush tips of two different colors, see how a third color is created when the second color is applied over the first.

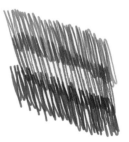

▲ Try some "feathering": lines that are laid down side by side. Notice the dark tone where the rows overlap. Leaving some white paper adds sparkle.

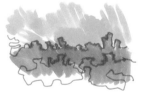

▲ Block in a light tone using the brush tip, then add a darker tone underneath. Work over the top right away with the fine point. The line remains crisp on dry paper, but where you touch the areas of blocked-in color, the line will "bleed."

Watercolors

If you practice the basic essential techniques needed to apply watercolors, you will quickly discover how the washes behave and how your brush, paper, and paint act together. These exercises use three colors.

▶ Wash

The color needs to smoothly graduate from dark to light. Practice on dry paper (as here) and on wetted paper. Gradually add more water to the color in your palette to make it lighter as you work up from the thicker and darker first stroke.

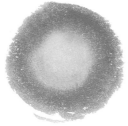
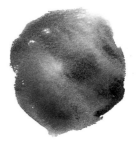

▲ Graded color wash

Work the same as the wash, but start at one side and blend in another color as you work over to the other side. Keep the paint watery.

▲ Soft and blended edges

Wet the whole area, and then add in a light center. Now slowly add darker colors to the outside, using plenty of water.

▲ Wet-into-wet technique

This is where you place wet colors onto a wet surface and let them diffuse into each other. Try rocking the paper back and forth.

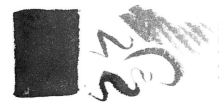

◀ Blocking in and brushstrokes

Fill in a square, blending to obscure the individual brushstrokes. Then apply a variety of strokes using a brush on its side, edge, and tip. Finally, dry the brush with a tissue and try some dry brushstrokes.

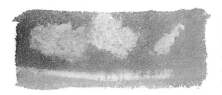

◀ Lifting out

To create an area of light within your watercolor wash, lift the area out using a dry tissue or brush. There will be some staining, and some papers are better than others for lifting out.

Masking fluid

This is used to block out selected areas of a painting when a wash is being applied over the top. It can be drawn on with an applicator (a ruling or drawing pen) in a tight and delicate design or flicked on with an old brush for a more random design. Add a drop of watercolor coloring to colorless fluid so that you can see where you have applied it. Dry thoroughly, add a watercolor wash, and let this dry before rubbing off the masking fluid with your fingers.

▶ Draw a design with masking fluid in a ruling/drawing pen. Let it dry, then wash over the top. Let this dry and rub off the masking fluid to reveal the first drawing on the white paper.

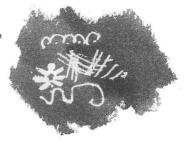

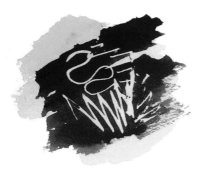

◀ Paint an undercoat in one color and let it dry. Apply a design in masking fluid, and once this is dry, wash over it with another color. When this has dried, rub away the masking fluid to display the drawing with the first color showing through.

Salts

Different salts give different effects when they are sprinkled into a very wet watercolor wash. This technique is fantastic for snow, seas, and foliage. Once the paint and salt are dry, the excess salt can be rubbed off.

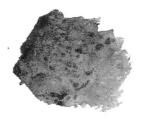

▲ A different design can be created using flake salt.

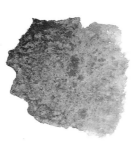

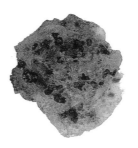

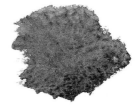

▲ Use table salt for these small, dotted markings.

▲ Create a mottled, sponged effect with rock salt.

▲ The pebbled design is formed with dishwasher salt.

Mixed media

Now try mixing your media. As you can see from the illustrations below, you can create wonderful effects, which will lead to some exciting and vibrant sketches. We have tried a few different options. Do not be afraid to experiment in order to discover even more.

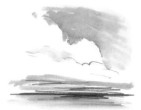

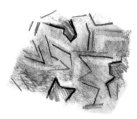

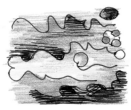

▲ Make some lines with a pencil and then use the brush tip of a watersoluble art pen over the top. The lines here suggest sky and cloud, so blue was chosen. The brush marks were diffused with clean water.

▲ Use the side of a piece of charcoal first, flat against the paper. Blend the marks with a finger. Then use black and sanguine conté over the top. Then finally, pick out light shapes with a tiny piece of putty eraser.

▲ Make some lines with the fine tip of an art pen. Then use some colored pencils gently over the top. Begin with your lightest colors. Where you overlay the colors, subtle new ones will be created.

▲ Create a block of color with the brush tip of an art brush pen. Then "dissolve" the marks with water, using a paintbrush. Use pastel pencils over the top, feathering the lines so that the underneath color shows through.

want to know more?

Take it to the next level . . .

Go to . . .
▶ Composition—page 36
▶ Foreground and distance—page 40
▶ Light, shade, and shape—page 42

Other sources
▶ Art stores
  try different materials
▶ Art classes
  many colleges offer painting courses
▶ Specialist magazines
  The Artist's Magazine, American Artist
▶ Publications
  visit www.harpercollins.com for
  HarperCollins art books

composing

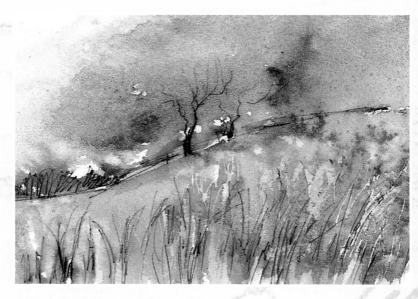

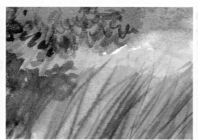

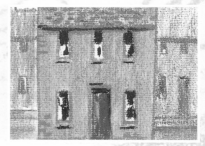

a picture

This chapter gives you some helpful ideas about depicting light and shade for believable shape and form and organizing your images to make a picture that "works." Understanding the basics of what constitutes a good design will help you create a more considered image that has impact and is strong and visually pleasing.

Composition

There are times when you want to sketch a whole scene or produce a sketch with a plan of making a painting of that subject at a later date. Composing a picture is not always easy. Every part of the picture has to be considered—not just the objects within the scene, but also the spaces between the objects. Composition is how you put together all these parts in order to make a satisfying whole.

Making a viewfinder

The first thing you need will become one of your most useful tools. It is a viewfinder. Every time we turn our heads, even a little, we see more and more of a view—and it can be hard to know where to begin and what to include. A viewfinder helps single out a section of a view, and it shows us what the picture might look like.

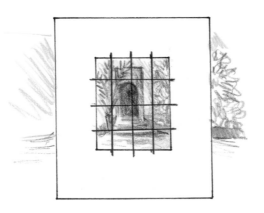

◀ You can cut out a viewfinder from a piece of stiff cardboard. The minimum size should be 4 x 6 inches (10 x 15 cm). Some artists find it helpful to tape lengths of black string across their viewing window, to create a grid. This makes it easy to check the position of objects in relation to each other.

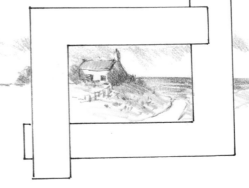

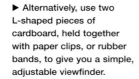

▶ Alternatively, use two L-shaped pieces of cardboard, held together with paper clips, or rubber bands, to give you a simple, adjustable viewfinder.

Creating a focal point

A good way to begin a sketch is to decide on a center of interest—technically known as a focal point—and then place this focal point on one of the "eyes" of the rectangle that you see through your viewfinder. This concept has been used by artists throughout the ages, after discovering that the viewer's eye naturally gravitates to these points. It is based on a fairly complex formula, but the principle can be simplified in this way.

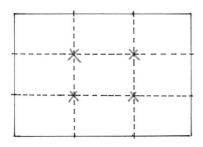

◀ Divide your rectangle into thirds. This will create four points where the lines intersect, and any one of these points is a perfect spot to place your focal point.

▶ The focal point of this sketch—the house that is nestling in the hills—sits perfectly on the top left "eye" of the rectangle.

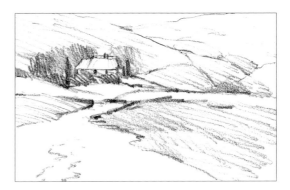

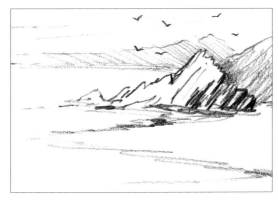

◀ Here, the jagged rocks are the main subject of the picture, placed on the top right "eye" of the rectangle. This makes the picture feel nicely balanced.

Counterchange

You can stress the importance of your focal point by using strong, dramatic contrasts—setting the lightest part of the picture against the darkest part, or vice versa. This use of light against dark and dark against light is called counterchange; it is very effective, and you should look for opportunities to use it whenever you can. Do not be afraid to exaggerate nature a little if it helps to do so.

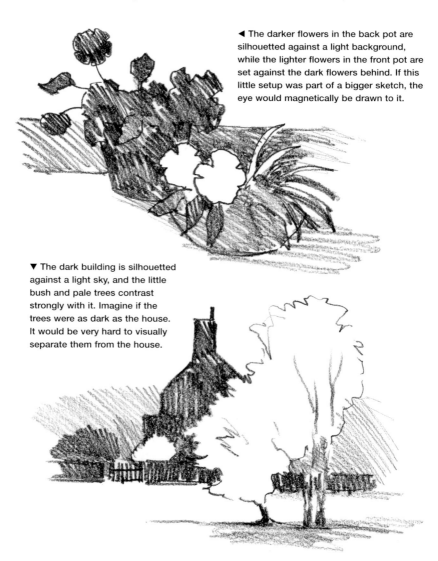

◀ The darker flowers in the back pot are silhouetted against a light background, while the lighter flowers in the front pot are set against the dark flowers behind. If this little setup was part of a bigger sketch, the eye would magnetically be drawn to it.

▼ The dark building is silhouetted against a light sky, and the little bush and pale trees contrast strongly with it. Imagine if the trees were as dark as the house. It would be very hard to visually separate them from the house.

Dos and don'ts

Here are a few pictorial dos and don'ts to consider.

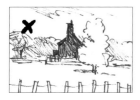

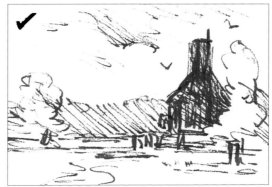

Don't place your focal point in the middle of the picture and try not to divide your picture in half. Also, don't block off the picture with a fence or wall at the bottom.

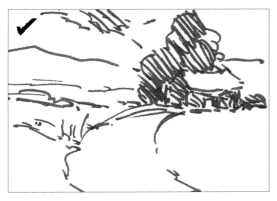

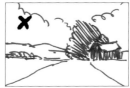

Beware of corners—they can act like arrows leading the eye out of the picture. The picture on the left is far more "comfortable," and we are led directly to the focal point.

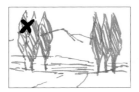

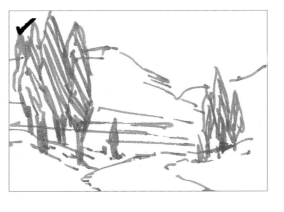

Although it's good to have similar shapes in a picture that can echo each other, vary their proportions and don't create "bookends" at each side of a picture with shapes of equal size.

Foreground and distance

**A piece of paper is two-dimensional—it only has width and
height. The challenge of painting is creating the illusion of
depth, giving it the three-dimensional appearance of reality.
You can do this by employing both differences in scale and
advancing (warm) and receding (cool) colors.**

Identical objects

To practice creating an impression of depth in your picture, it is best to begin
by experimenting with objects that are of identical size and a simple shape.

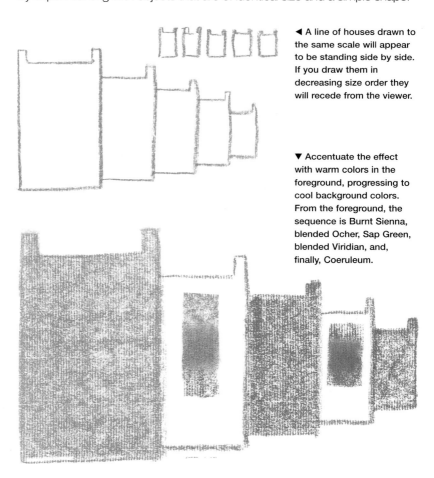

◄ A line of houses drawn to
the same scale will appear
to be standing side by side.
If you draw them in
decreasing size order they
will recede from the viewer.

▼ Accentuate the effect
with warm colors in the
foreground, progressing to
cool background colors.
From the foreground, the
sequence is Burnt Sienna,
blended Ocher, Sap Green,
blended Viridian, and,
finally, Coeruleum.

► Here the houses are arranged more informally. Each one stands on a baseline, and as they recede, the intervals between the baseline diminish.

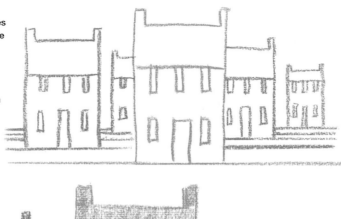

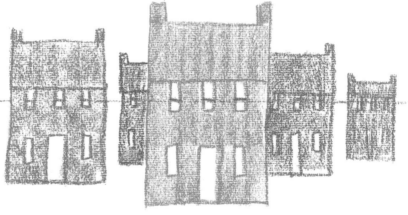

▲ The blue line represents your eye line, which in this instance is from an upper window. It shows that the houses are of a similar size and are on level ground. Such construction lines can be erased when they are no longer needed.

▼ Detail and contrast become more indistinct with distance. It helps here to view the subject with your eyes half closed.

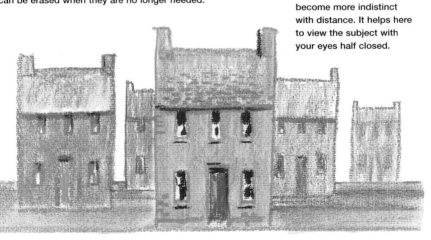

Light, shade, and shape

The depiction of light and shade (tone) helps the viewer's eye recognize objects and adds solidity to their form. However, painting is made easier if you ignore the question of tone and concentrate on finding the basic shapes of the objects at first.

From squares to cylinders

Shapes distort when viewed from above or below, so it is advisable for beginners to choose a central eye line, indicated here by a blue line.

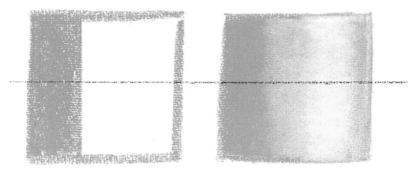

❶ A precise demarcation of flat tone would turn this square into a cube, whereas the

gradual blending of tone will change it into a cylinder (right).

❷ For a cylindrical shape, start by painting a wide band of color. You can then add progressively darker or lighter narrowing bands to each side (left) and blend them.

You can see how solid color gives the appearance of a matt surface (center), while leaving some white paper gives a glossy effect (right).

Triangles, pyramids, and cones

Like squares, cubes, and cylinders, triangular shapes distort when seen from an angle. Again, choose a central view as shown here by the blue line.

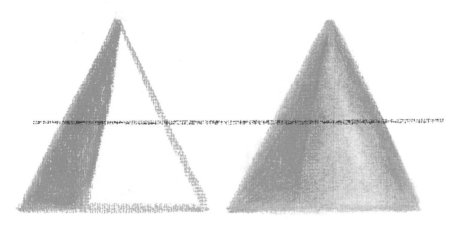

❶ This triangle looks like a pyramid when it is divided into two flat areas of tone (left).

With the tone gradually blended, the same shape becomes a cone (right).

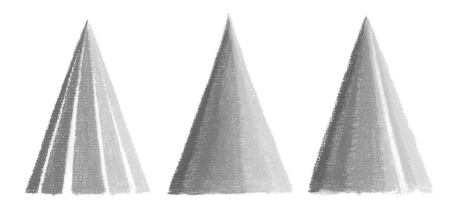

❷ Tonal changes radiate from the top of a cone. Place the widest central band of color first, followed by the lightest and darkest tones to each side (left). Blend the colors,

completely covering the paper entirely for a matt surface (center) and allowing some white paper to show through to give the appearance of a glossy surface (right).

Circles and spheres

Unlike square and triangular shapes, circular objects retain their shape no matter which position they are viewed from. Consequently, there is no need to establish a particular eye level.

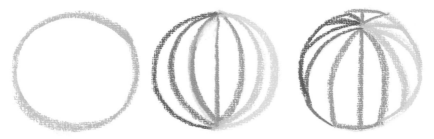

❶ Draw a circle, then add sections on each side of a central axis (center) or radiate

them out from any point, flattening them on the opposite side (right).

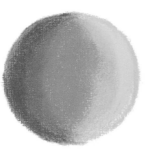
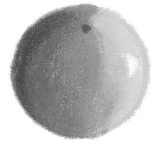

❷ Fill in the colors, graduating the tone and completely covering the paper for a matt surface (left) or lifting a highlight for a glossy one (right).

❸ The angle of light from the top of an object to its baseline will determine the length of a cast shadow. The illustration on

the left shows the shadow cast at noon. In the illustration on the right, the time could either be mid-morning or mid-afternoon.

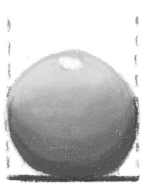
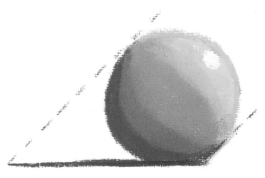

Combining shapes

Most objects consist of a combination of triangular, rounded, or squared shapes. Make diagrammatic drawings of domestic items, paying attention when you are establishing your eye level (shown here by a blue line).

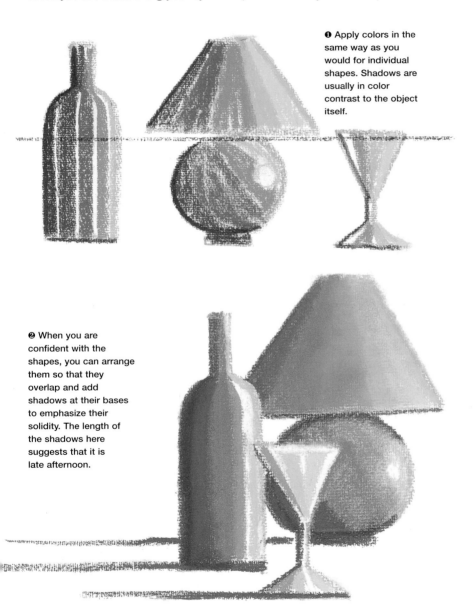

❶ Apply colors in the same way as you would for individual shapes. Shadows are usually in color contrast to the object itself.

❷ When you are confident with the shapes, you can arrange them so that they overlap and add shadows at their bases to emphasize their solidity. The length of the shadows here suggests that it is late afternoon.

Making objects 3-D

Most objects are three-dimensional—so we have to find a way to translate three dimensions into a flat, two-dimensional drawing. Drawing the outline of the object isn't enough to give the impression of three dimensions—the "form" of the object. Shadows will help describe the form—sometimes the object will have lines "within" it that will help too.

Form

Try copying this example. Then find similar objects at home and draw them using the same principles to describe the three-dimensional form. Use a 2B pencil for this sketch.

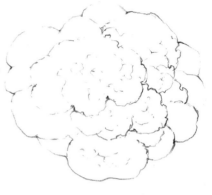

❶ Here is a simple, amorphous shape. It could be anything—it could certainly be flat, like a coaster. Or it could be a hole!

❷ Some "internal" lines have been added. The object now has form—it is full, round, and has bumps. Notice how the overlapping lines portray the cauliflower's form. Also, see how the lighter lines on the left give the impression of light falling onto the object.

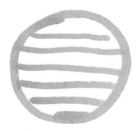

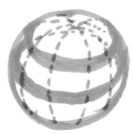

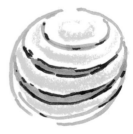

▲ How you draw your "internal lines" makes a difference, too. See how straight lines give the impression of a flat surface.

▲ Placing a series of curved lines both up and around the circle makes it feel like you are looking at a round object.

▲ The series of lines thicken as they come toward you: if they were exaggerated at the front, the ball would appear to be more curved.

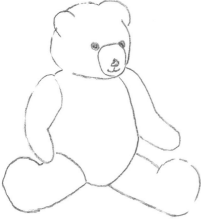

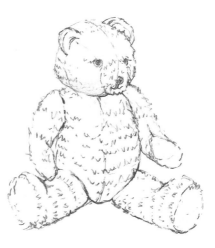

❶ The outline (in red conté) is almost enough to tell us that the toy teddy bear is fat and rounded. However, the line here is monotonous, making him look more like a cartoon bear.

❷ In this drawing the small lines used to show the bear's fur curve around his shape. The central line, used to define the shape of his head, has been left; this helped plot his features in the correct place.

Shadows

When light falls on an object, it will usually cast a shadow. That shadow will help describe the shape of the object.

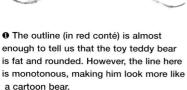

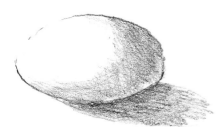

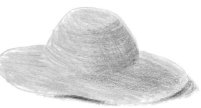

▲ The shape of the egg quickly becomes easy to see when a strong light from the left casts a shadow. "Tone," which is just another word for shading, was scribbled in, using the side of a 2B pencil held almost flat against the paper.

▲ See how the shape of the hat comes to life in three dimensions when the shadow is added. The blue lines curve around the hat's crown, reinforcing the impression of roundness, while straighter blue lines are used for the shadow on the brim. Wax pencils were used for this sketch.

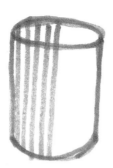

◄ This cylinder appears flat, as the shadows are not correct.

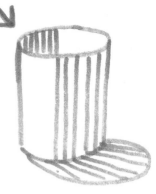

► Draw in an arrow as a reminder of the light source, then readjust the shadows. Remember that light against dark shows form and shapes and will make an object look 3-D.

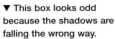

◄ This carrot looks like a cylinder on its side. A darker line has been drawn under it, giving it a feeling of weight and stability.

▼ This box looks odd because the shadows are falling the wrong way.

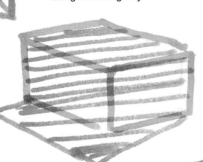

▲ The shadows have been corrected to give the box contrast and depth.

► The present has a ribbon that wraps around the whole shape, giving it form. The decoration colors appear light in the shadows and dark in the light. This also helps with the realism.

COMPOSING A PICTURE

48

Edges

Be careful not to draw a hard line all around your subject, unless you are drawing an "edge." Developing an awareness of the difference between an "edge" and continuous form is important.

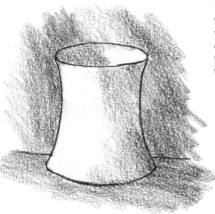

◀ In this conté drawing the outline of the vase was drawn, then the tone, or shading, was added. The lines used to show the top and bottom edges of the vase are fine, but those describing the sides of the vase seem to bring them forward.

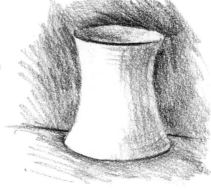

▶ A line is used for the front top edge and bottom edge of the vase, but the dark tone behind "describes" the sides of the vase, improving the illusion of a curving form.

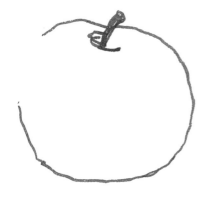

❶ The apple was drawn with a watersoluble art pen, deliberately leaving a broken line on the left in order to suggest light falling on the fruit from that side.

❷ The line was then wet, teasing the color out to form a shadow on the table top, and leaving white paper in order to suggest the lightest part of the apple.

One subject—different approaches

An excellent way to explore the wide range of material mixtures is to try out one subject in a variety of ways, moving it around compositionally. This example uses the corner of a cornfield. Each composition emphasizes the different ways in which you can tackle one subject. By brightening, darkening, or detailing one point, or by introducing an undulating line, the eye is carried to a different part of the picture.

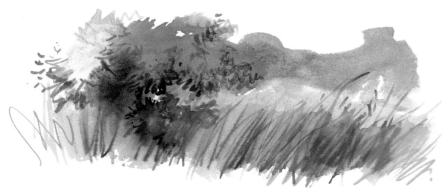

▲ The sky, background, and tree are flowed in with washes of colored inks on wet paper. When it is partially dry, the corn and tree details are added with fiber-tip pens.

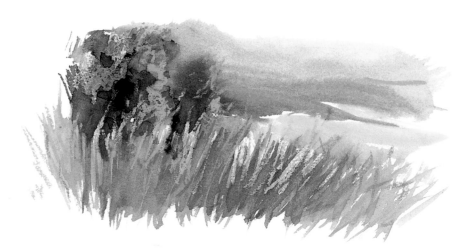

▲ The texturing of the cornfield is applied with pale oil pastel. Using several colors makes the contrast more exciting when watercolor washes are applied.

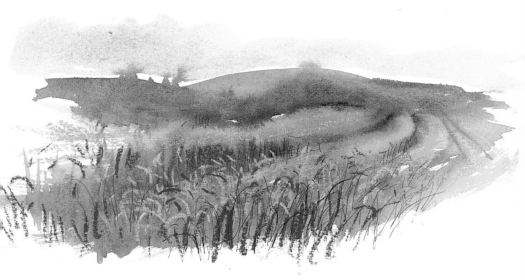

▲ The distant feel is created by using a watercolor base, separating and darkening the foreground. Waterproof ink and soft pastel give the highlights and details, and the foreground ears of corn are enlarged to reinforce the feeling of space.

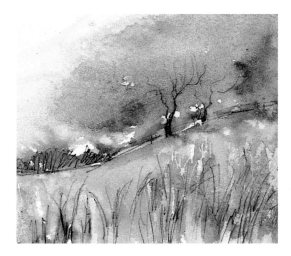

▲ Nonwaterproof black ink details of the trees, grasses, and distant hills are washed over with watercolor. While it is still very wet, salt is dropped into the watercolors, mottling the trees with the mid-distance and foreground corn. When it is totally dry, the salt is rubbed off and then a few more grasses are added to the foreground.

want to know **more?**

Take it to the next level . . .

Go to . . .
- ▶ **landscapes**—page 136
- ▶ **buildings**—page 166
- ▶ **the seaside**—page 176

Other sources
- ▶ **Photographs**
  useful sources of reference
- ▶ **Art shows**
  look out for local or national events
- ▶ **Internet**
  interactive CD-ROMs
- ▶ **Publications**
  visit www.harpercollins.com for HarperCollins art books

fruits and

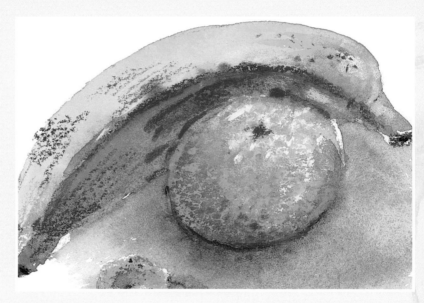

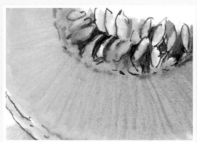

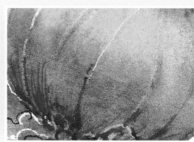

vegetables

Fruits and vegetables are the most wonderful things to draw. They have natural form: shapes that are organic and flowing, not man-made and rigid. They offer plenty of color and variety of texture too. Although most oranges may form perfect spheres, other fruits and vegetables will have particular shapes, so observe them closely.

Drawing fruits

In this chapter we will look at some of the most important elements of drawing—how to begin, combining objects, creating texture, and assessing proportions. Fruits and vegetables are great starting points for learning how to sketch. Because they are natural forms, they all differ, so we have to look really hard to find the correct shape.

Pear

Although a 4B pencil was used for this drawing, you can use any grade of pencil for this exercise. Work lightly to start with.

❶ Pears are great fun to draw. Start off by drawing the shape with a 4B pencil. A broken line may help give you confidence.

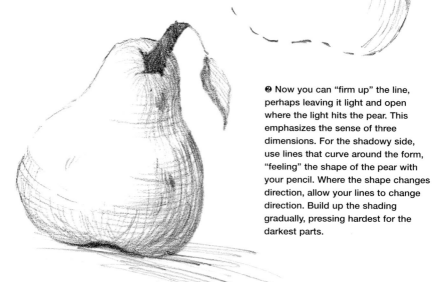

❷ Now you can "firm up" the line, perhaps leaving it light and open where the light hits the pear. This emphasizes the sense of three dimensions. For the shadowy side, use lines that curve around the form, "feeling" the shape of the pear with your pencil. Where the shape changes direction, allow your lines to change direction. Build up the shading gradually, pressing hardest for the darkest parts.

Nectarine and banana

Now put two fruits together, one overlapping the other, to practice putting objects together convincingly. This time, a piece of charcoal is used.

❶ Using the point of the charcoal, begin with the outlines of the fruits. Where one fruit is behind the other, follow the line through, to ensure that the drawing makes sense.

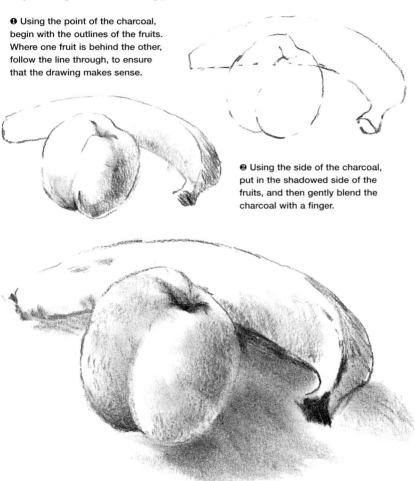

❷ Using the side of the charcoal, put in the shadowed side of the fruits, and then gently blend the charcoal with a finger.

❸ Add the shadow on the tabletop, looking hard to see which is darker, the shadow or the fruit. Build up the form of the fruits. Add any tiny details, such as markings on the banana. If you want to "lift" any unwanted charcoal to refine the drawing, use a tiny piece of putty eraser. When you finish, spray the drawing with some fixative. (Notice the tiny area of reflected light on the shadowy underside of the nectarine. When you place an object on a light surface, reflected light often bounces up onto it.)

Strawberries

It is not necessary to draw with a graphite pencil and then color in your sketch. Working directly with a colored pencil will immediately capture the color of the fruit.

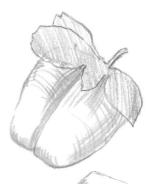

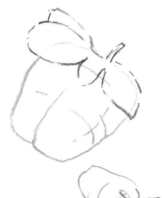

❶ Begin by drawing the main shapes of the strawberries. Sketch the outline and also some internal lines to show fullness, crevices, and where the shape changes direction.

❷ This time, begin with the darker areas and use directional strokes to explain the form, curving around the fruit and down the sides.

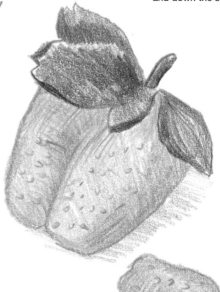

❸ Gradually build up the color, leaving slightly paler areas where the light strikes the strawberries and their leaves. Tiny semi-circles suggest seeds. Use short strokes of green for the shadow on the tabletop.

Colored pencils

red-orange   green

Painting strawberries in mixed media

Strawberries always make my mouth water. Their textured surface makes them interesting to paint. The leaves are a delightful contrast, like a green hat!

Watercolors

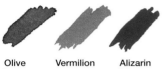

Olive   Vermilion   Alizarin
Green   Crimson

Soft pastels

orange   pink

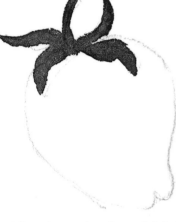

❶ Draw the strawberry in pencil. Paint in the top using green mixed with a little Vermilion.

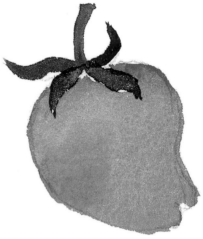

❷ Block in the fruit shape with Vermilion.

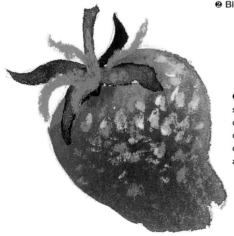

❸ While the paint is still wet, drop in some Alizarin Crimson to darken the color to show form. When it is completely dry, apply dots of soft orange and pink pastels. Spray with a fixative if required.

Orange

Oranges are simple in shape, and painting one is relatively easy. However, you need to take care with the textured feel of the skin, as casual stippling could have a flattening effect. Notice how the stippling on the fruit is flatter and thinner at the circumference.

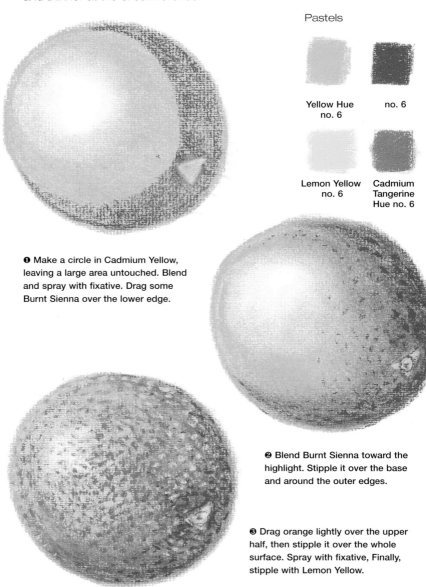

Pastels

Yellow Hue
no. 6

no. 6

Lemon Yellow
no. 6

Cadmium
Tangerine
Hue no. 6

❶ Make a circle in Cadmium Yellow, leaving a large area untouched. Blend and spray with fixative. Drag some Burnt Sienna over the lower edge.

❷ Blend Burnt Sienna toward the highlight. Stipple it over the base and around the outer edges.

❸ Drag orange lightly over the upper half, then stipple it over the whole surface. Spray with fixative, Finally, stipple with Lemon Yellow.

FRUITS AND VEGETABLES

58

Plums

Plums have no pattern to describe their shape and no obvious texture. But if you look carefully, you will often find that the skin has a bloom to it. This is texture in its subtlest form, shown by gently dragging a light color over a dark one.

❶ Drag a short length of red pastel in two overlapping ovals, then overlay this with a partial outline in purple. From some viewpoints a plum displays distinct halves.

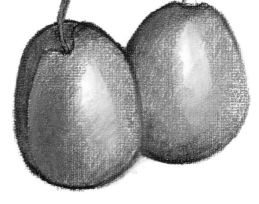

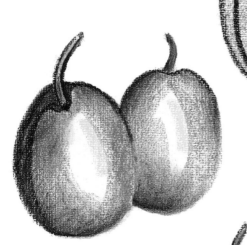

❷ Add yellow in the highlights. Extend and deepen the red. Blend purple into the red, but maintain the crease. Draw yellow over the purple stalks in order to create a mix.

Pastels

Crimson
Lake no. 4

Mauve
no. 5

Lemon
Yellow
no. 6

French
Ultramarine
no. 1

❸ Drag orange lightly over the upper half, then stipple it over the whole surface. Spray with fixative. Finally, stipple with Lemon Yellow.

FRUITS AND VEGETABLES

59

Shiny cherry

First of all, let's try a very simple project: creating a shine on these cherries using four different techniques, each one giving a slightly different result.

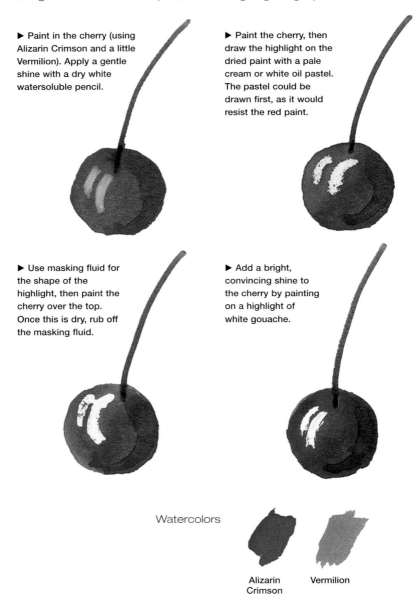

▶ Paint in the cherry (using Alizarin Crimson and a little Vermilion). Apply a gentle shine with a dry white watersoluble pencil.

▶ Paint the cherry, then draw the highlight on the dried paint with a pale cream or white oil pastel. The pastel could be drawn first, as it would resist the red paint.

▶ Use masking fluid for the shape of the highlight, then paint the cherry over the top. Once this is dry, rub off the masking fluid.

▶ Add a bright, convincing shine to the cherry by painting on a highlight of white gouache.

Watercolors

Alizarin
Crimson

Vermilion

Rosy apple

Apples vary a lot in their color and patterns, and they are relatively easy fruit to paint. However, you can make them more of a challenge by cutting them in half to expose the core with its seeds.

Watercolors   Pencils

Cadmium   Vermilion   violet   crimson
Yellow

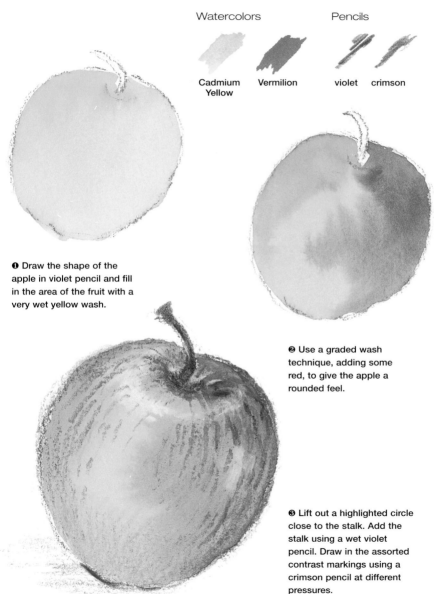

❶ Draw the shape of the apple in violet pencil and fill in the area of the fruit with a very wet yellow wash.

❷ Use a graded wash technique, adding some red, to give the apple a rounded feel.

❸ Lift out a highlighted circle close to the stalk. Add the stalk using a wet violet pencil. Draw in the assorted contrast markings using a crimson pencil at different pressures.

Fruit sections

Cutting fruits into segments will give you unfamiliar shapes. This is a good way of training eye–hand coordination. Try hard to get the proportions right, just by using your eye. Conté was used for these sketches.

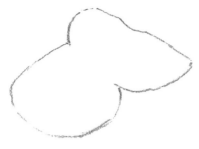

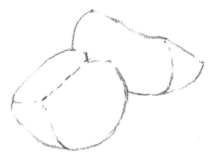

❶ Cut an apple into segments. Place two pieces together, and before beginning to draw them, blur your vision by squinting so that you can only just see the pieces. Looking at them in this way will eliminate detail and fuse the two shapes into one, larger shape. Try drawing the outline of the two together, looking hard at the shape created where they overlap.

❷ When you are satisfied with your large shape, look to see where the "planes" of the segments change. The top, central line of my front segment was not in the center, as you might have expected.

❸ Finish off the sketch by putting in the tones of the shadowed sides of the fruit and the shadow on the table. The table shadow is darker than the fruit shadow.

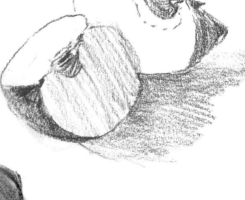

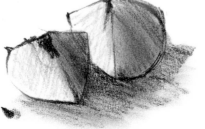

◀ These tiny segments—one quarter cut in half again—do not look at all like an apple, but you just have to draw what you can see.

Mouthwatering melon

By cutting this fruit open, you will be painting a different, more complicated shape, and adding the details of the seeds, flesh, and skin.

Pen   Pencils

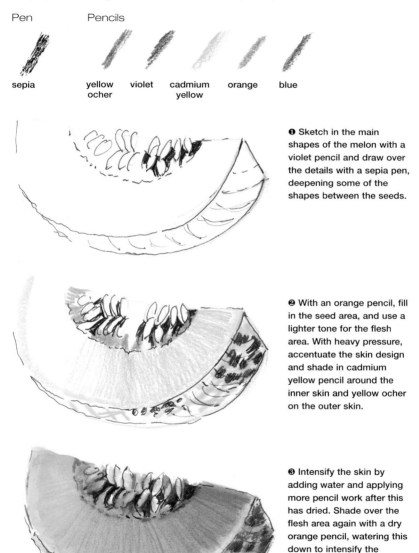

sepia   yellow   violet   cadmium   orange   blue
             ocher   yellow

❶ Sketch in the main shapes of the melon with a violet pencil and draw over the details with a sepia pen, deepening some of the shapes between the seeds.

❷ With an orange pencil, fill in the seed area, and use a lighter tone for the flesh area. With heavy pressure, accentuate the skin design and shade in cadmium yellow pencil around the inner skin and yellow ocher on the outer skin.

❸ Intensify the skin by adding water and applying more pencil work after this has dried. Shade over the flesh area again with a dry orange pencil, watering this down to intensify the texture and color. Anchor the image down using a blue pencil wash and some loose scribbles for the shadows beneath.

EXERCISE ## Sketch a fruit still life

You can copy this sketch, but then you will find it rewarding to set up your own still life, using similar fruits. If strawberries are not in, use any other small fruits to give a change of scale from the larger pieces.

The palette
4B pencil

 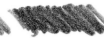

lightest tone   medium tone   darker tone   darkest tone

❶ Set up the fruits with the light coming from one side. Using a 4B pencil, lightly sketch the outlines of the fruits. It helps to straighten out curved lines a little, as shown here. It can also help to create an imaginary "grid" in your mind's eye, or even hold up your pencil, to see where the objects line up with each other.

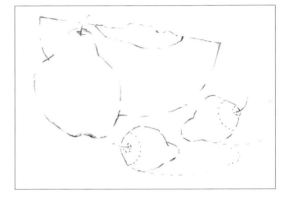

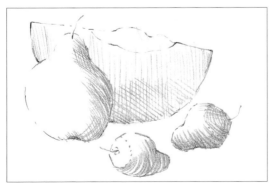

❷ Now half close your eyes and squint at the setup. Begin to develop the tone (shading) on the fruits, starting with the darker sides. This should give the fruits three-dimensional form immediately. Try to make your lines "wrap around" the curved fruits.

❸ Continue to develop the forms of the fruits by adding more shading, looking carefully in order to define the darkest parts—for example, the shadows under the fruits. Add the shadows on the tabletop. Begin to define some detail, such as the tiny leaves on the tops of the strawberries.

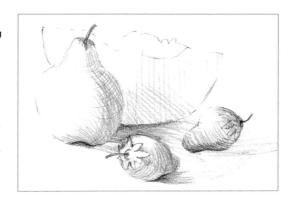

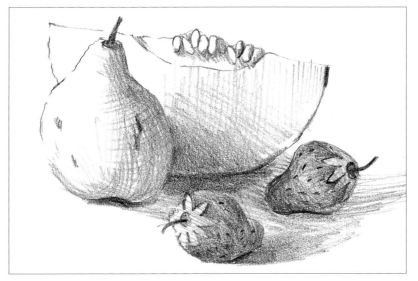

❹ Gradually add more shading. You can take this step as far as you like, even using the side of the pencil lead to close up the lines and darken areas. Finish off with details—the seeds on the melon and the texture on the strawberries.

MUST KNOW

Improve your powers of observation

Because most fruits and vegetables are so familiar, it is very easy to fall into the trap of generalizing about their shapes and drawing what we THINK is there, instead of observing them very closely and then drawing exactly what we see. If you know that you are inclined to generalize, you should try to break this habit in order to improve your powers of observation.

EXERCISE Paint fruits in mixed media

This is a simple, but interesting, combination of fruits to paint, since the fruits vary in color and texture. Once you have tried this combination, you can try choosing a different variety and then painting them with the same materials.

The palette

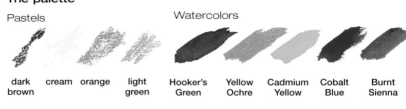

Pastels

Watercolors

| dark brown | cream | orange | light green | Hooker's Green | Yellow Ochre | Cadmium Yellow | Cobalt Blue | Burnt Sienna |

❶ Draw the fruits with a blue pencil. When you are painting a group of objects, place them together in an interesting pose, perhaps wrapping one around the other or overlapping them.

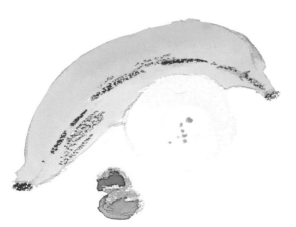

❷ Press cream pastel onto the side of the tangerine and add orange pastel markings for the texture. Draw a little light green pastel on the grapes and dark brown pastel to show the banana markings. Paint the banana Cadmium Yellow and the grapes green.

❸ Paint the tangerine in Yellow Ocher and complete the spots with orange pastel. Deepen the shadowed area on the banana with brown paint. Use light green pastel at both ends of the banana and accentuate its markings with additional dark brown pastel.

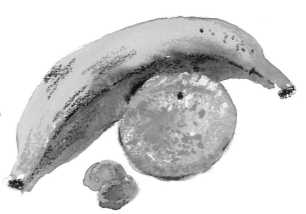

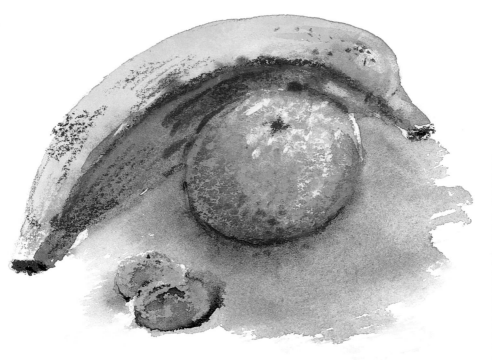

❹ Paint around the fruits with a blue wash. Wash brown paint into the tangerine to heighten the texture marks.

▶ Drawing vegetables

Raid your fridge for a few vegetables to draw. Vegetables come in so many varieties and so many different shapes and colors. You could devote a lifetime to drawing them!

Onion

The golden rule—although this term is used loosely because there are no "rules" about drawing—is form before texture. In other words, make the object look three-dimensional before you allow yourself to tackle the fun part—the surface texture.

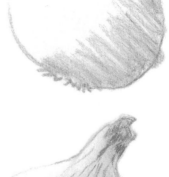

❶ An orange pastel pencil was chosen for this lovely golden-orange onion. First, draw the shape of the onion, and then scribble some tone onto the shadowed side.

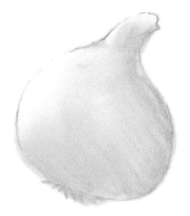

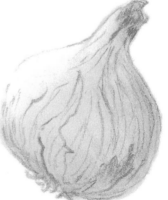

❷ Using a finger, gently blend the pastel strokes into the paper to create the full, rounded form of the onion. If your blending doesn't look exactly right, you can remove some color with a putty eraser.

❸ Finally, add the texture of the onion skin. By pressing hard, you can suggest the edges of broken skin, while lightly drawn lines, following the form of the onion, imply the "lines" on the onion.

Papery onion

Onions are an excellent example of the way lines can be used to define and accentuate a structure, as well as to add texture. Try not to overgeneralize; carefully observe the lines before you draw them in, for an authentic look.

Watersoluble pen   Watercolors

sepia   Yellow   Burnt   Cerulean
         Ochre   Sienna

❶ Draw the onion with a pencil. Apply masking fluid in lines that separate out and give the onion a good, rounded shape, and then wiggle in some roots. Apply a little watersoluble sepia pen to the top and bottom.

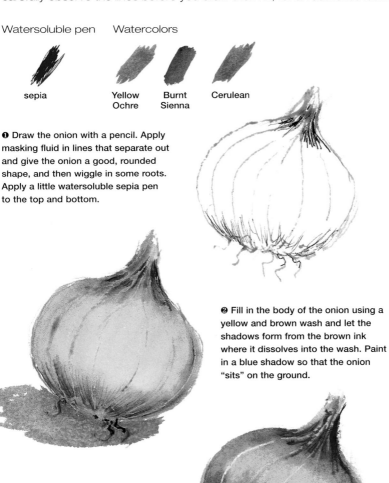

❷ Fill in the body of the onion using a yellow and brown wash and let the shadows form from the brown ink where it dissolves into the wash. Paint in a blue shadow so that the onion "sits" on the ground.

❸ When it is dry, rub off the masking fluid and use the sepia ink to redraw some of the lines and roots.

Mushroom

Judging proportions using your eye isn't easy—check them by using artists' measuring. Hold out a long pencil, with your arm straight and your elbow locked. Point the pencil at the ceiling (when checking height) or at the wall to your left or right (for width), not the object. Close one eye, line the top of the pencil up with the top of the object, and place your thumb on the pencil in line with the bottom of the object. This becomes your measuring unit—use it to check all of the other parts in relation to this unit as you draw.

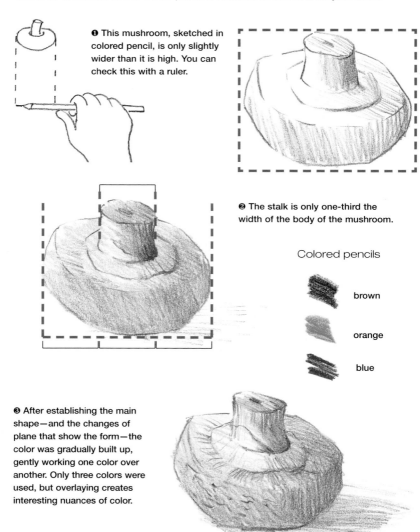

❶ This mushroom, sketched in colored pencil, is only slightly wider than it is high. You can check this with a ruler.

❷ The stalk is only one-third the width of the body of the mushroom.

Colored pencils

brown

orange

blue

❸ After establishing the main shape—and the changes of plane that show the form—the color was gradually built up, gently working one color over another. Only three colors were used, but overlaying creates interesting nuances of color.

70

Yellow pepper

Peppers are also interesting to paint, since their surface is brightly colored and shiny. After you've copied this one, try painting one cut in half, to show the intricate interior and the seeds.

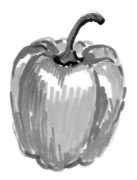

❶ Draw the basic pepper shape and its curved stalk in pencil. Now emphasize the deep crevices with red fiber-tip pen and then color in the stalk with the light and dark greens.

❷ Complete the shape by coloring it in with yellow, using orange for the deeper shaded areas.

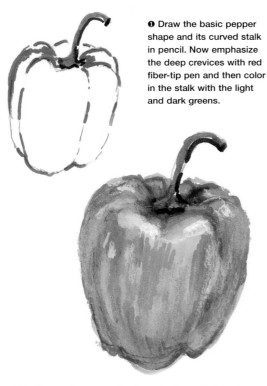

❸ Wash over the pen work with water to gently blend the colors. When it is dry, add highlights to the top and edges using cream and white pastels.

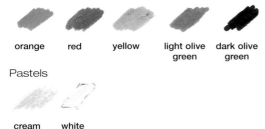

Fiber-tip pens

| orange | red | yellow | light olive green | dark olive green |

Pastels

cream   white

want to know more?

Take it to the next level . . .

Go to . . .
▶ shapes and patterns—page 74
▶ sketching plants—page 86
▶ drawing trees—page 102

Other sources
▶ Photographs
   useful sources of reference
▶ Art shows
   excellent for inspiration and ideas
▶ Sketchbooks
   good for improving observational skills
▶ Painting vacations
   expand your horizons with other artists
▶ Publications
   visit www.harpercollins.com for HarperCollins art books

natural

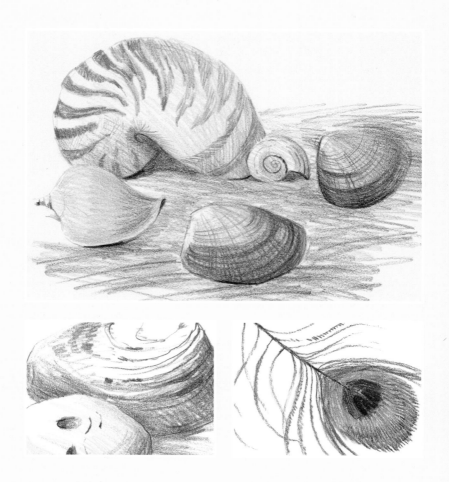

forms

You do not have to go far in order to find natural forms. A walk in your garden or along the seashore will provide some inspirational objects—stones, rocks, pieces of bark, pebbles, roots, feathers, shells, and seaweed. These may not be as pretty as flowers or as colorful as vegetables, but they are still fascinating to draw. Collect interesting objects to sketch.

73

Shapes and patterns

As you sketch natural forms, you will become aware that nature is a wonderful artist. Many natural objects have beautiful shapes, colors, and patterns, and sketching these will train you to investigate how things are made, as well as how they look. Start with relatively simple items and build up your confidence to tackle more complex forms.

Pebbles

These two pebbles were smooth and round, and one seemed to have a built-in, circular pattern, that echoed its shape. If you look hard to find the natural rhythm of construction and see how the pattern follows the form, this will help a great deal. The danger is drawing the patterns as if they were on a flat surface, which flattens the object.

Colored pencils

lemon yellow	purple	dark green-blue	green	blue

❶ Begin with the basic outline, using colored pencils. Where the pattern is the strongest, indicate this with some circular lines that follow the form. You can also add a little tone to establish the 3-D form.

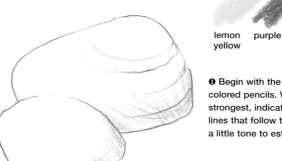

❷ Gradually add more color; one pebble is more yellow than the other, which is gray-green. As you build up the color, try to suggest the pattern while following the form. Finally, put in the little dents and cracks in the front pebble, and then you can add the shadow underneath them.

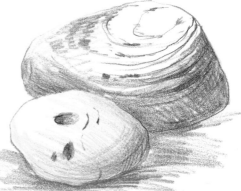

Feathers

Pastel pencils, sharpened to a fine point, were used for these drawings. Sharpen a pastel pencil by gently rubbing it on some fine sandpaper. Press lightly when you are sketching, otherwise the point will break.

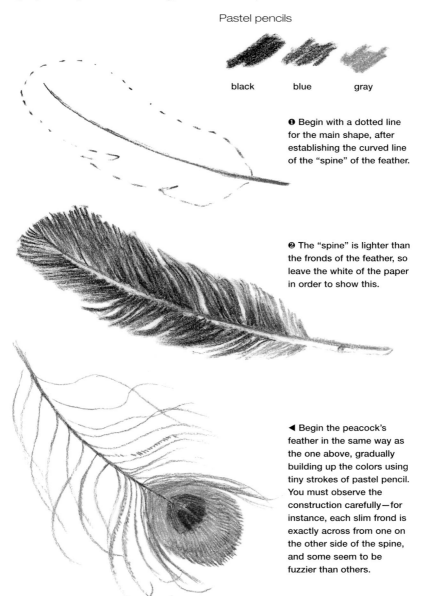

Pastel pencils

black   blue   gray

❶ Begin with a dotted line for the main shape, after establishing the curved line of the "spine" of the feather.

❷ The "spine" is lighter than the fronds of the feather, so leave the white of the paper in order to show this.

◀ Begin the peacock's feather in the same way as the one above, gradually building up the colors using tiny strokes of pastel pencil. You must observe the construction carefully—for instance, each slim frond is exactly across from one on the other side of the spine, and some seem to be fuzzier than others.

Tree bark

Sketching bark will train you to observe well, but it will also train you to simplify because it is almost impossible to include every tiny crack and flake. The pattern is complex, and if you do not follow the form in places, you could flatten the shape and lose the sense of three dimensions.

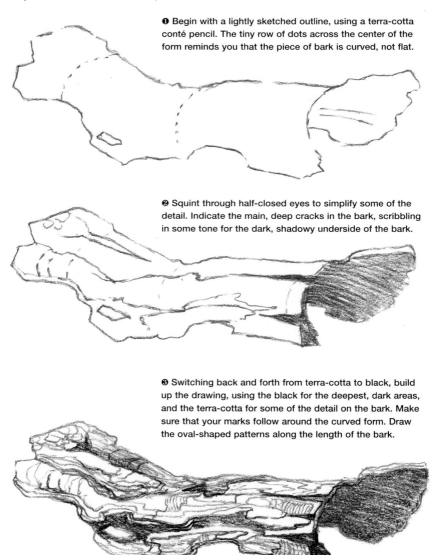

❶ Begin with a lightly sketched outline, using a terra-cotta conté pencil. The tiny row of dots across the center of the form reminds you that the piece of bark is curved, not flat.

❷ Squint through half-closed eyes to simplify some of the detail. Indicate the main, deep cracks in the bark, scribbling in some tone for the dark, shadowy underside of the bark.

❸ Switching back and forth from terra-cotta to black, build up the drawing, using the black for the deepest, dark areas, and the terra-cotta for some of the detail on the bark. Make sure that your marks follow around the curved form. Draw the oval-shaped patterns along the length of the bark.

Seedpod

A thin stick of charcoal with a point was used for these drawings. To keep the point on your charcoal, gently run it across a piece of fine sandpaper.

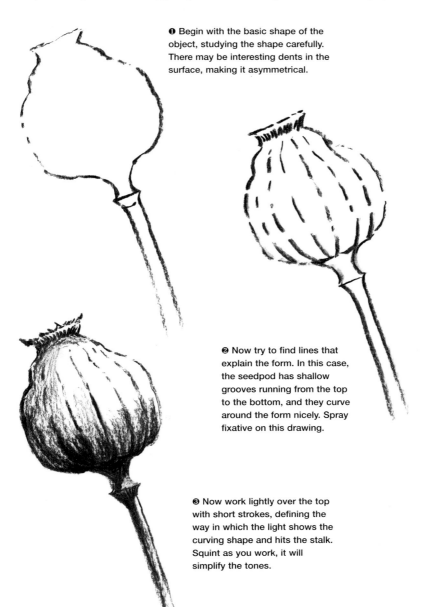

❶ Begin with the basic shape of the object, studying the shape carefully. There may be interesting dents in the surface, making it asymmetrical.

❷ Now try to find lines that explain the form. In this case, the seedpod has shallow grooves running from the top to the bottom, and they curve around the form nicely. Spray fixative on this drawing.

❸ Now work lightly over the top with short strokes, defining the way in which the light shows the curving shape and hits the stalk. Squint as you work, it will simplify the tones.

Shells

Shells are delightful to look at and a treasure trove for the painter. Collect a few shells from the beach or from the wonderful selections in many seaside gift stores, and try out this exercise using different shapes. This is another example of approaching the same subject using different media.

▶ Here the shells are inked in using an art pen with a sepia watersoluble pencil drawing. A little purple watercolor is washed over, and more pigment is added to the shadows. Pale Yellow Ocher is painted into the shell's grooves.

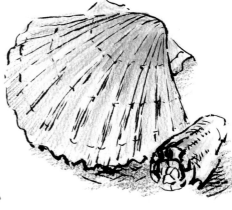

◀ The main skeleton is drawn in using a brush pen, then colored using dry orange, purple, and yellow watersoluble pencils, scribbling them in to give a loose hint of color.

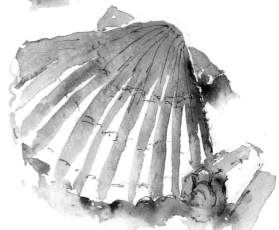

▶ Orange and violet watercolors are painted into the main shape, emphasizing the texture and structure. Ultramarine is added to the shadows.

Limpets

Shells add interest to water subjects or a still life and are attractive objects on which to practice pastel painting. Find some shells and explore their shapes and growth patterns. Limpets have contour lines like hills on a relief map, but the periwinkle is a free-flowing spiral.

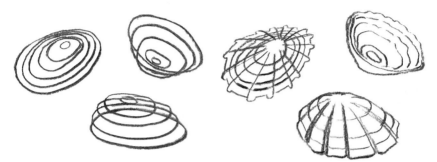

❶ Draw the contours from above, underneath, and from the side with charcoal, carefully following the form of the shell.

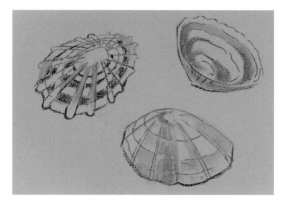

❷ Lightly draw visible contours and radiating lines in purple-gray. Fill the closer ridges and one inner contour with the darker raw sienna. Blend some of the purple-gray on each shell.

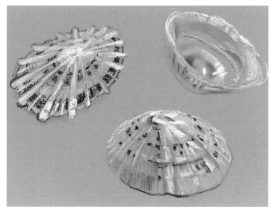

❸ Add the lighter raw sienna. Place purple-gray spots on the front shell and infill the spaces on the gray shell with coeruleum, then add the white highlights.

Discover Drawing and sketching

EXERCISE # Drawing shells with wax pencils

Shells can be found in many different shapes and sizes. Instead of drawing them one at a time, put a few together, using shells with similar, harmonious shapes, so that they work well together visually. Consider their placement carefully—overlap their forms in places, look at the spaces between them, and create an interesting and balanced design. An uneven number of shells will provide a better design than an even number.

The palette
Wax pencils

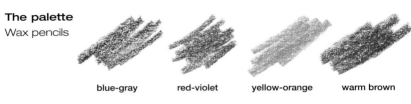

blue-gray   red-violet   yellow-orange   warm brown

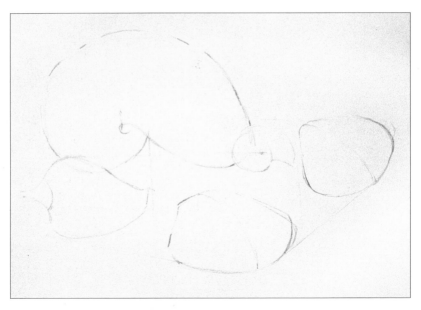

❶ For this picture, you should use colored wax pencils. Begin with the outlines of the shells, checking the positions of the shells in relation to each other. If you look carefully, you might see the faint lines that are used for this purpose.

NATURAL FORMS

80

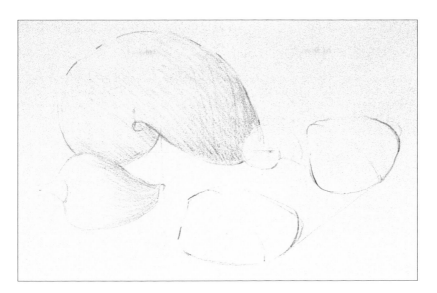

❷ Add tone to show the shadow side of the shells—the light was coming from above and to the left. For the smaller shell on the left, curve the lines to follow the form. For the big shell, simple crosshatching will suffice, since the pattern is strong and this will come later.

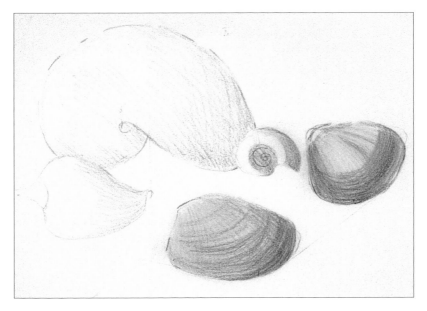

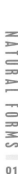

❸ Next, work on the three remaining shells. You should use blue-gray on the smaller shell at the back of the group and a mixture of blue-gray and red-violet on the purple shells. Make sure that your marks curve around the form.

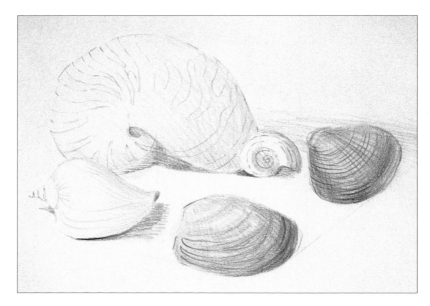

❹ You can use some simple outlines to show the patterns on the shells, then begin to suggest some of the shadows underneath them.

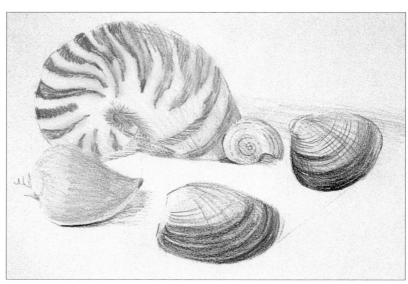

❺ Complete the pattern on the largest shell. The pattern breaks up into lines, and the tone varies from solid and dark to lighter and finer. Add some yellow-orange to the shell on the left, which is a warmer color, and emphasize the pattern on the purple shells.

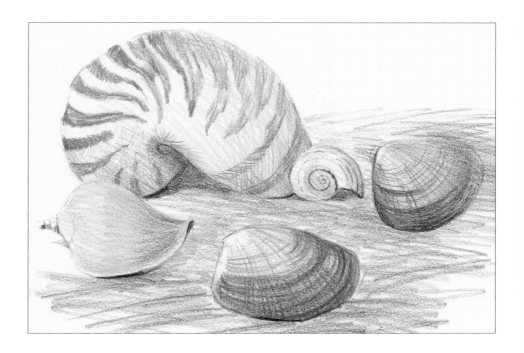

❺ Finished picture: Tinted watercolor paper, 6½ x 10 inches (17 x 26 cm). Where the shells meet the ground, there is a dark line; the pattern on the purple shells can be exaggerated a little, and distant lines curve over the shell to suggest the form. A little blue-gray stroked across the large shell helps the bottom part recede. Lines of blue-gray, red-violet, and yellow-orange are used for the ground on which the shells sit.

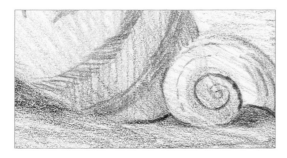

This detail clearly shows how the pattern "sits" on the top surface of the shells, following the curving form. Even the small shell has a shadow to show the "dip" in the shell.

want to know more?

Take it to the next level...

Go to . . .

▶ **sketching plants**—page 84
▶ **drawing trees**—page 102
▶ **seaside sketching**—page 178

Other sources

▶ **Photographs**
  useful sources of reference
▶ **Art shows**
  provide inspiration and ideas
▶ **Sketchbooks**
  good for improving observational skills
▶ **Gardens**
  research new painting subjects
▶ **Publications**
  visit www.harpercollins.com for HarperCollins art books

plants and

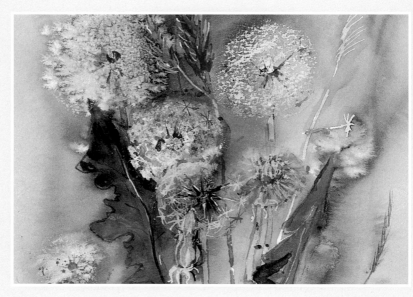

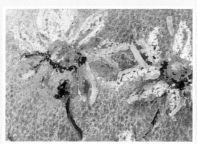

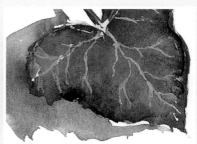

flowers

Throughout the ages artists have drawn plants and flowers. We can see the influence of floral forms all around us, in decorative carvings, ironwork, architectural detail, jewelry, and fabrics. Their complexity and beauty provide us with a wealth of material, whether we want to produce botanically accurate images or capture their essential essence.

► Sketching plants

Flowers have naturally undulating, rhythmic lines, and you should try to get a little "flow" in your sketches when you tackle their lovely forms. This doesn't mean that you should sacrifice close observation. You are training your eye and your hand. Gradually, fluency will come, and, with it will come the ability to work more freely. Without the underpinning of good observation, "free" sketches can become sloppy.

Cosmos: open face

Start with some simple, open-faced flowers, such as this Cosmos, before you try more complex, many-petalled flowers that are more difficult to sketch. A flower with a simple circle of petals around its center may seem easy to draw, but it will provide more than enough challenges for a novice artist. Its structure may be straightforward, but you will still need a sharp eye and a sensitive hand in order to capture its essence in a portrait.

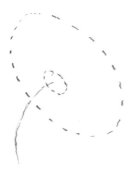 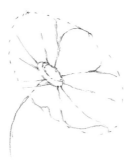 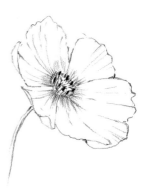

❶ Close your eyes halfway to find the main, overall shape. Now find the position of the center of the flower and see where the stalk meets the petals—it often helps to follow it through. A 4B pencil has been used for this simple line drawing.

❷ Drawing a flower slightly turning away from you is much more interesting than drawing it facing you. After establishing the structural shape, carefully place the petals, looking hard to see where they overlap, which describes their positions.

❸ Finally, study the beautiful, varied edges of the petals and try to represent them accurately. Fine lines radiating out from the center show where the petals are curved and where they are straighter, describing the form without shading.

Cosmos: underside

The undersides of flowers are also fascinating to study, in order to see how the petals attach to the stem. This is the underside of a Cosmos.

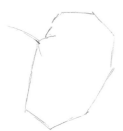 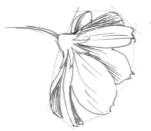 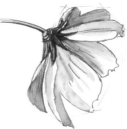

❶ Instead of using a simple, oval form, look at the flower through half-closed eyes and then draw a box with straight edges to represent the positions of the petals.

❷ Draw the flower with the firm point of a watersoluble art pen. Where the petals are in shadow, you can use additional lines to describe the darker tone.

❸ "Loosen" the ink on the darker parts of the petals with a brush and water. When dry, erase your pencil lines and redraw any ink lines that have been washed away.

Lilac

For this "slightly"-more-flowing sketch, use only four colored pencils—green and orange for the stem and leaves, and two purples for the flowers.

Colored pencils

green   orange   dark purple   light purple

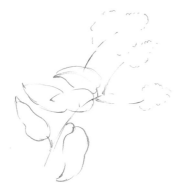 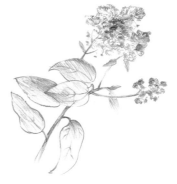

❶ Begin with the stem, sweeping the lines all the way through and behind any leaves. See how the leaves join the stem, and then give free rein to flowing, linear curves.

❷ Hint at the veins on the leaves, since they describe the form. Use dots, dashes, and little curving lines for the tiny purple flowers, picking out the odd stem in places.

Mixing greens

When you paint plants and flowers using watercolors, you need different greens. Use some of the ready-mixed greens, such as Hooker's, Sap, or Viridian, and then mix in a little Cadmium Yellow or Naples Yellow for the lightest greens; Cerulean, Cobalt Blue, or Burnt Sienna for mid-tone greens; and deep Violet, Alizarin Crimson, or deep brown for the darkest greens.

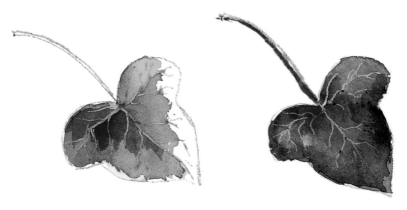

❶ Draw in the basic shapes in pencil and put masking fluid on the veins and the stalk. Start painting a red wash over the dried masking fluid and then, over the top, paint green with a little yellow.

❷ Continue to paint the entire leaf and stalk, adding more green to the edges of the leaf. This will make them darker in tone and give an impression of a slight curl on the edge of the leaf.

Watercolors

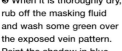

| Alizarin Crimson | Olive Green | Cadmium Yellow | Cobalt Blue |

❸ When it is thoroughly dry, rub off the masking fluid and wash some green over the exposed vein pattern. Paint the shadow in blue.

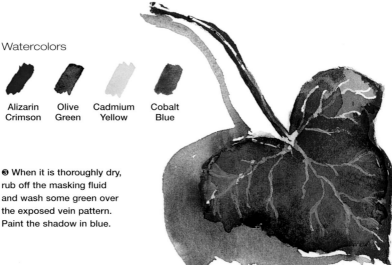

Simple leaves

Choose three tones of one color for this basic leaf shape. Yellow-green has been used here, but red or orange would be equally as appropriate, since leaves can be found in a wide variety of colors and tones.

The crease along the central spine of a leaf creates a division of light and shade. Draw the shape first, fill with cross-hatching, and then spray it with fixative (left). Next, draw the veins alternately on each side, using dark on light and light on dark (center). If the surface is glossy, lift out highlights between the veins with an eraser (right).

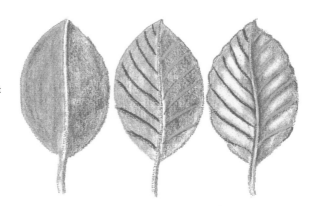

Curving leaves

Leaves often fold and curve, and, by doing so, they show both their upper and under surfaces. However, if you observe them carefully, curling leaves are no more challenging to paint than a flat leaf.

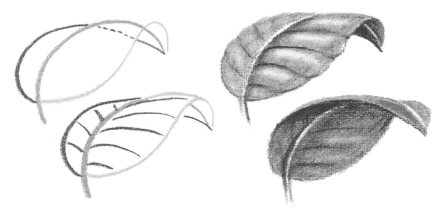

❶ Here, orange has been used to show how the spine of the leaf decides the angle of its curl. A dotted line indicates the continuity of the unseen edge.

❷ To show the leaf curving toward you, instead of away, reverse the curl, using a darker green for the main body of the leaf to indicate the shadow on the underside.

Buds

Flower buds are enclosed in a casing of leaves that protect the petals and the seedpod. The volume of the closed bud also governs the shape of the subsequent seedpod.

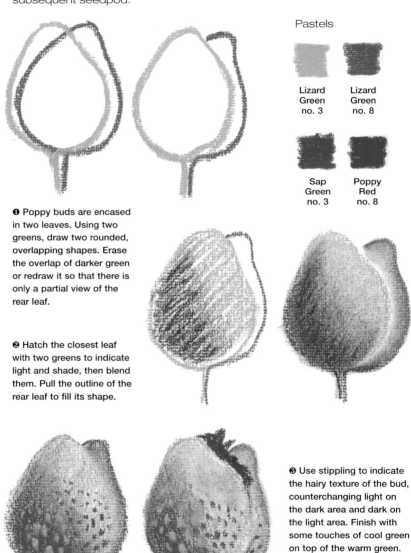

Pastels

Lizard Green no. 3	Lizard Green no. 8

Sap Green no. 3	Poppy Red no. 8

❶ Poppy buds are encased in two leaves. Using two greens, draw two rounded, overlapping shapes. Erase the overlap of darker green or redraw it so that there is only a partial view of the rear leaf.

❷ Hatch the closest leaf with two greens to indicate light and shade, then blend them. Pull the outline of the rear leaf to fill its shape.

❸ Use stippling to indicate the hairy texture of the bud, counterchanging light on the dark area and dark on the light area. Finish with some touches of cool green on top of the warm green. Add the red of a petal, dragging down the color between the leaves.

Petals

Petals appear in many forms, from the complex frills of dianthus to the simple, saucer shapes of buttercups. However, they are rarely completely flat, so pay attention to how the light falls on them and alters their color.

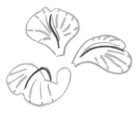
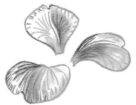
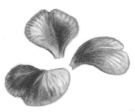

❶ Begin by drawing inwardly and outwardly curved petals, then a foreshortened view.

❷ Draw in pinks and yellows following the growth line out from the base of the petal. Blend in the same direction.

❸ The source of light is to the right. On the inwardly curved petal it strikes the opposite edge.

Tulips

Flowers have natural flowing shapes—and as you practice these shapes, your painting will become more fluid, and you will gain the confidence to work more freely. Tulip petals wrap smoothly around each other, and they are gorgeous to paint—especially when their heads start to droop.

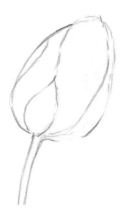
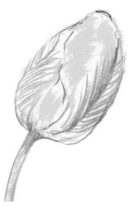
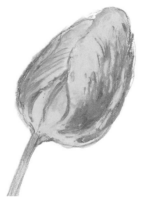

❶ Begin by drawing in the egg-shaped head of the tulip and the flow of the petals in vermilion pencil. Now add a pale green stalk.

❷ Add deeper colors and patterning by drawing yellow soft pastel and red pencil markings on each petal and green up the stalk.

❸ Wash over with water and let the colors mix. When dry, redraw the red and reapply the yellow to illustrate the form without shading.

Daisies

A many-petalled flower like the Michaelmas daisy is more difficult to draw than the broad petals on page 91, but you don't have to include every detail. Once you are familiar with its form, try painting the whole plant.

Pastels

Mauve no. 1   Mauve no. 5   Green Gray no. 1   Sap Green no. 4   Cadmium Yellow Hue no. 6

 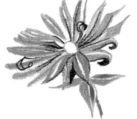 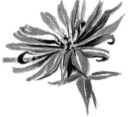

❶ Working upside-down, draw a gray-green stem from the base to the center. Turn it the right way up. Outline the petals in Mauve no. 1 and add the leaves.

❷ Erase the upper stem. Fill in the petals with Mauve no. 1 leaving some highlights. Use Mauve no. 5 for the shadows and then add some Sap Green to the leaves.

❸ Make yellow dots for stamens and surround them with Mauve no. 5. Blend the two Mauve colors on the petals but keep crisp edges on the petals facing forward.

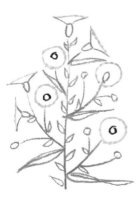 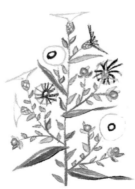 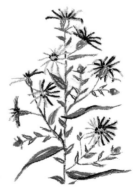

❶ Draw the stem in Green Gray Plot the flower heads so that they are seen facing, in profile, or from behind. Erase the outlines later.

❷ Side stems and junctions have extra leaves. Crisscross the seedpods and begin to add structure to the flower heads.

❸ Finally, you can flesh out the detail on the daisy flower heads, using a darker mauve to show where the shadow falls.

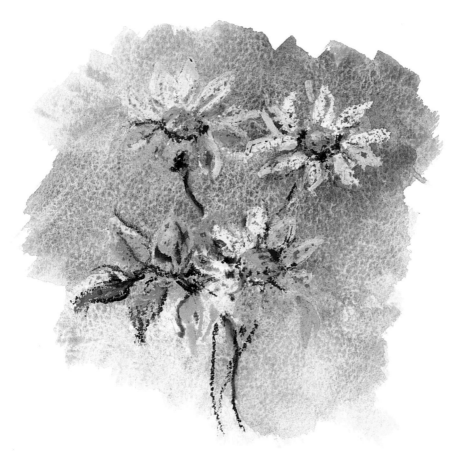

▲ Strong strokes of brown, cream, and orange oil pastels are used for the flower heads and burnt sienna, and light and deep green pastels for the foliage and stalks. A blue background is washed over it and the images stand out through the watercolor wash. Extra details may be added while it is still wet.

► Colored paper adds "mood" and gives the flowers an immediate tone. Yellow, white, cream, and light and dark green oil pastels are used for the stalks and the foliage. A dark wash of Olive Green and blue-green over the background allows the colored paper to gleam through, uniting the picture.

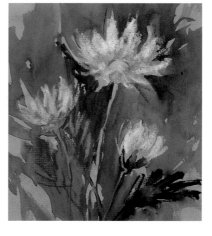

Poppies

Poppies are charmingly attractive with their hairy stems, ragged leaves, and unkempt, crumpled petals, but beneath the apparent untidiness and fragility of the flowers, there is a governing structure.

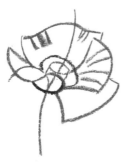 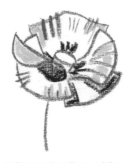 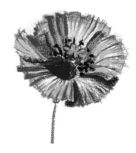

❶ Drawing begins where the stem, petals, and seedpod meet. This is easier to see when one petal is removed.

❷ Draw red outlines, adding creases for the petal curves. Use darker red for shaded areas; yellow for highlights.

❸ Add in the stamens, then wiggle a line across the edges of the petals in order to indicate the frills.

Pastels

| Sap Green no. 4 | Poppy Red no. 8 | Indian Red no. 6 | Cadmium Yellow Hue no. 6 |

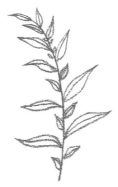 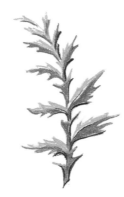 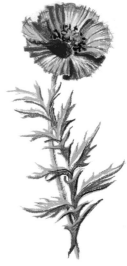

❶ You will find that it is easier to paint spiky poppy leaves if you look at the underlying structure and stem first. They become smaller toward the top. With tracing paper, follow the lines of your initial drawing.

❷ Add spiky edges to the leaves and draw smaller leaves across the stem, in order to indicate twists and turns. Now fill in the greens, using a darker tone on the underside of leaves where they are in shadow.

❸ Combine the flower and leaves. Overlay it with the leaf stem, balanced in the opposite direction. Develop the leaf with a third green, keeping an open texture. Add hairs to the stem by scratching with a scalpel.

Using watercolors

Understanding how a flower is constructed is vital when painting. The way that the petals fit together and blend or contrast is characteristic of a particular flower. The background determines the flower's tone and colour.

Pencil
Watersoluble ink
Watercolors

burnt sienna   sepia   Yellow   Olive   Vermilion   Magenta
                                 Ocher   Green

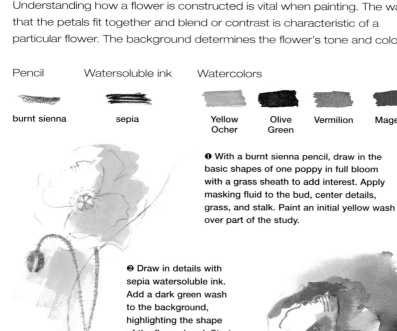

❶ With a burnt sienna pencil, draw in the basic shapes of one poppy in full bloom with a grass sheath to add interest. Apply masking fluid to the bud, center details, grass, and stalk. Paint an initial yellow wash over part of the study.

❷ Draw in details with sepia watersoluble ink. Add a dark green wash to the background, highlighting the shape of the flower head. Start adding Vermilion to the flower.

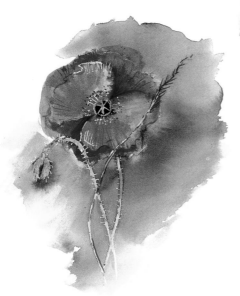

❸ While it is still wet, add Magenta and more Vermilion to the whole flower head and bud, letting it diffuse the ink and run slightly into the other colors. Add petal creases and grass texture with more sepia ink. Rub off the masking fluid and soften the white patterns with light yellow, green, or watery Vermilion.

Dandelions

Some flowers are at their most interesting at the seed stage, such as this dandelion. Try copying this example, then experiment with a similar flower that is in seed, such as an "old-man's beard" or a poppy head.

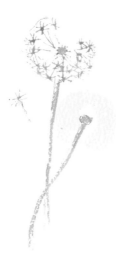

❶ Draw in the two heads, placing masking fluid details on one stalk and drawing a circle of cream pastel on the second stalk. Apply pink oil pastel to the stalks.

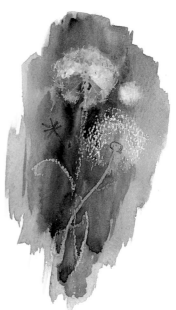

❷ Weave a little thread of green and orange oil pastel through the background as trailing weeds. Now mix a dark green and mid-green background watercolor wash, and then apply it over the picture.

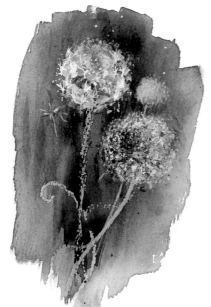

❸ When it is thoroughly dry, rub off the masking fluid. Splatter some white gouache over the flower heads to soften the effect. Draw in the remaining details with a dry brown pencil.

Watercolors   Pencil

Olive   Green   brown
Green   Gold

Oil pastels

cream   pink   pale   orange
green

Grouping flowers

Painting a couple of heads of the same type of flower gives you the opportunity to combine proportions, tones, colors, and shapes.

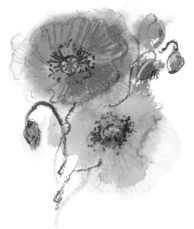

◀ The soft "halo" effect on the poppies was created by wetting the edges with water before starting to paint the petals. One flower is more dominant and colorful, and the other is like a softer silhouette.

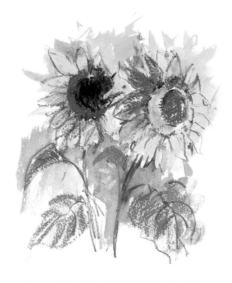

▶ These sunflowers are in contrasting but complementary tones. The leaves are drawn in emerald and Olive green soft pastels, the flower petals and centers in orange, burnt sienna, and brown. Yellow watercolors give the basic flower color, and some details are outlined with a brown pencil. For the leaf texture, pastels are added to dried watercolor.

Dandelion heads

Here, several of the same variety of seed heads were created by using different painting methods, plus the flower, leaves, and buds. It is a delightful array of mixed media.

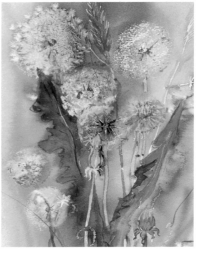

▶ The top left seed head is created by using salt sprinkled into the dark background while it is still wet. Cream oil pastel on the top right seed head resists the wash. The shape of the central, bluish seed head is dabbed out using a tissue and splattered with some white gouache. The random seeds (dandelion clocks) are created with salt dropped into the wet background and allowed to dry before working on them.

EXERCISE Pot of flowers in pastel

Tackling a small still life—a few simple flowers in a little plain pot—is a great
way to give yourself confidence before trying a more ambitious, large vase
of flowers—or even a corner of your garden in full bloom. Cut the flowers
short, so that their petals overlap the lip of the pot.

The palette Pastel pencils

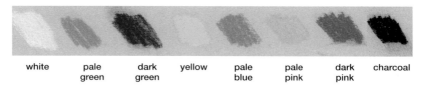

| white | pale green | dark green | yellow | pale blue | pale pink | dark pink | charcoal |

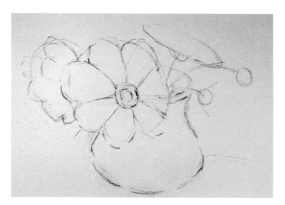

❶ On soft gray pastel paper,
using charcoal, sketch the
shapes of the flower heads
—circles and ovals. Look at
where the centers are—the
center of the big flower was
slightly off-set to the right.
Define the shapes of the
petals carefully, adding lines
of charcoal at the base
where the color is very dark.
Charcoal can easily be
rubbed off with a putty
eraser, so don't hesitate to
correct any mistakes.

❷ Spray the drawing with
fixative before adding any
color. Work from light to
dark. Use pale pink for the
lightest parts of the flower
heads, and pale green for
the lightest parts of the
stems and the leaves on
the buds.

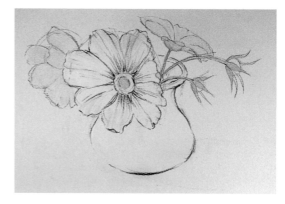

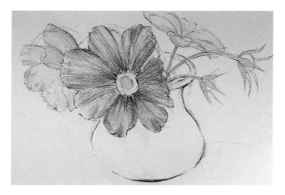

❸ Use the darker pink for the main flower. Make some long and sweeping marks, following the form from the center to the outer edge. Petals often have little ridges that beautifully describe their form . Notice how the pastel pencil marks blend with the charcoal.

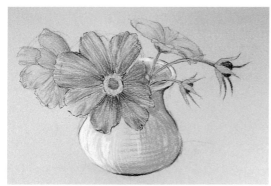

❹ Use white for the left side of the pot and pale blue for the side in shadow. Curve the marks around the pot from the top to the bottom and from right to left. When the shadow is complete, use pale blue on the light-colored flower heads at the back, to hint at shadows.

want to know **more?**

Take it to the next level . . .

Go to . . .
▶ **drawing trees**—page 102
▶ **planning landscapes**—page 138
▶ **seaside sketching**—page 178

Other sources
▶ **Photographs**
   useful sources of reference
▶ **Art shows**
   look out for local or national events
▶ **Gardens**
   will provide subjects and ideas
▶ **Painting vacations**
   expand your horizons with other artists
▶ **Publications**
   visit www.harpercollins.com for HarperCollins art books

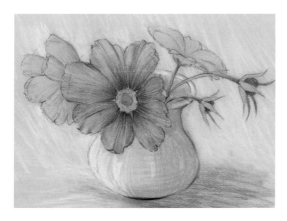

❺ Finished picture: Pastel paper, 8 x 11 inches (21 x 28 cm). Add a shadow on the ground with charcoal and pale blue over the top. Press hard on the darkest parts of the petals with dark pink. Scribble some white behind the pot and flowers to suggest a background. Spray with fixative.

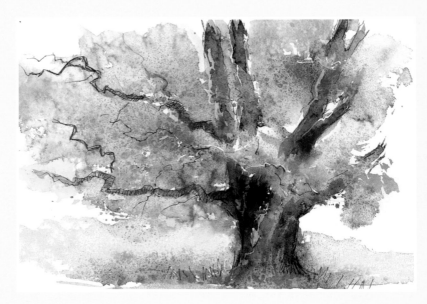

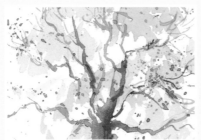

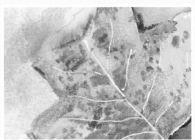

trees

To draw trees in all their forms and varieties, you will have to understand their structure and be able to capture their essential shape, as well as something of their life force. They all have the same basic structure, but they are often shaped by their experiences, and they have an individuality that makes every tree different and unique.

Drawing trees

To make trees convincing, the basic structures of the trunk, branches, twigs, as well as the leaf textures and colors, all need to be studied carefully. Observing a deciduous tree in the winter is the easiest time, since they become more daunting when they are clothed in a mass of foliage.

Basic steps

There are three main stages of drawing a tree successfully. First, you will need to observe the outline, then the pattern, and finally, the structure.

Outline

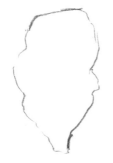

Start with the basic outline. Even within the same variety, trees tend to differ.

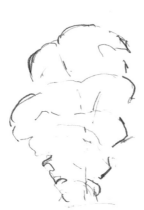

Pattern

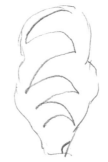

Look closely at the patterns within the tree: how do the lines within the tree flow?

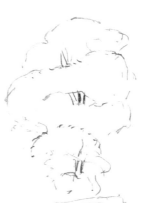

Structure

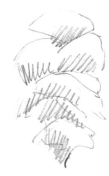

Elaborate the structure by defining the areas of light and shade.

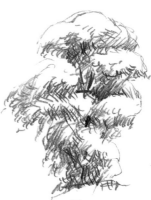

Tree trunk

It is fun to study trees. As well as having different shapes, their textures vary too. A 4B pencil was used for these drawings. You can also try making sketches like these in conté and in pastel pencils.

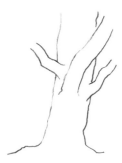 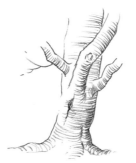 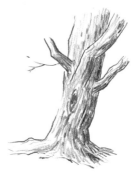

❶ Begin with a tree trunk. Notice how the tree flares out at the base, how the branches connect to the trunk, and that most branches remain the same width until they fork.

❷ Add curving lines running around the form. As you look up the tree, the curves arc upward; looking down, the curves swing down. The lines curve under the branches and dip into the hollows.

❸ Suggest bark with parallel strokes, some light and some heavy. Heavier marks on the right and under the branches suggest round forms revealed by light from the left and above.

Tree bark

A tree's trunk is its protective armor. Tree trunks can be smooth, deeply fissured, metallic-surfaced, peeling in strips, or thick and fibrous in texture. The amazing variety is breathtaking. Like the leaves, the trunk is characteristic of the variety of the tree and needs careful observation.

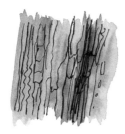 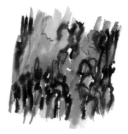 

▲ Sycamore: The lines and rectangles in the bark are detailed in assorted shapes and sizes using a black waterproof pen. This is covered by a gray and violet watercolor wash.

▲ Scotch pine: Circles and ovals are painted in orange, brown, and yellow watercolors and diffused with a watersoluble pen in sepia. When it is dry, the definite shapes are drawn in.

▲ Silver birch: Watersoluble pencils create slender lines of yellow ocher, gray, and browns to connect the abstract dark brown shapes. A wash is added to soften the contrasts.

Branches

A vital thing to notice about tree branches and twigs is that they do not actually taper. This is a common misconception. Look closely, and you will see that branches grow for a distance and then throw off smaller branches that themselves throw off even narrower twigs.

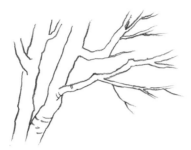

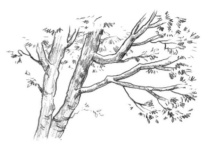

❶ Begin by drawing branches carefully, observing both the width of the branch and the changes of contour and direction. Look at the shapes between the branches, this may help too. I sketched this in black conté.

❷ Now you can add leaves. You do not need to carefully draw every leaf—short, stabbing marks can be enough to suggest foliage. You could add the occasional complete leaf shape, since leaves vary from tree to tree.

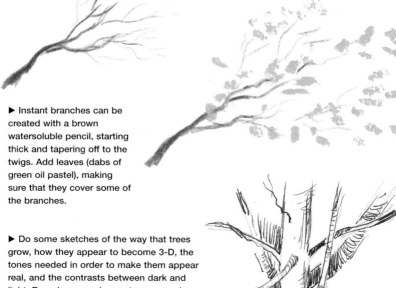

▶ Instant branches can be created with a brown watersoluble pencil, starting thick and tapering off to the twigs. Add leaves (dabs of green oil pastel), making sure that they cover some of the branches.

▶ Do some sketches of the way that trees grow, how they appear to become 3-D, the tones needed in order to make them appear real, and the contrasts between dark and light. Branches can change tone several times compared with others in the background and foreground. A blue steel-nibbed pen was used here.

Leaves and fruit

Outdoor sketches of overall shape can be done quickly, but botanical examples allow for leisurely study at home. Such details are unnecessary for painting an entire tree, but they give vital understanding of the subject.

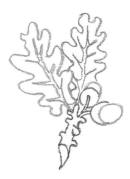 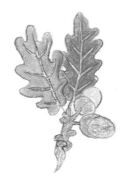 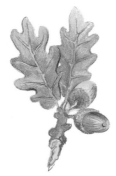

❶ Draw outlines in colors that are characteristic of each set of berries, cones, buds, and flowers. Notice how they compare with each other in scale.

❷ Fill in the outlines, extending the color range. This shows both summer and fall leaves on one twig, but ideally you should make separate seasonal studies.

❸ Complete the study by blending and overlaying using stronger colors. Be aware of tonal contrasts of light and dark, saving highlights from the start.

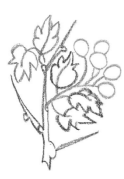 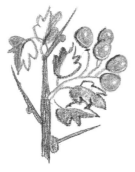 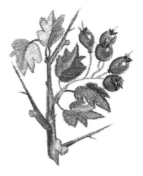

❶ Using the same method as above, draw details of a less densely foliaged tree, such as a hawthorn. Small, sparse leaves on a twig indicate a tree that has only a light canopy of foliage .

❷ Next, you can lightly fill in the leaves with some color, leaving half of each. Next, fill in the berries, too, but make sure that you save the highlights on them.

❸ Complete the filling in of the leaves, intensifying tonal contrasts. Strengthen the berries, being careful to preserve their highlights. Finally, you can add the long, spiny thorns.

Fall leaves

Fall brings new challenges for the artist. You will love painting the colors of this season: russet, oranges, reds, yellows, and browns.

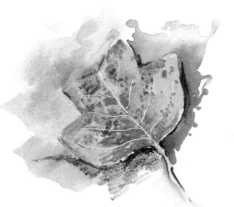

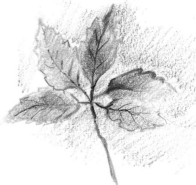

▲ Masking fluid is used for the pale veins, and wet watersoluble pencils are mottled together for the leaf surface. Traditional yellow pastels are applied to show sections where the leaf is drying.

▲ The different parts of this leaf are sketched in dry watersoluble pencils, with small details in sepia waterproof pen. The violet, orange, pink, and red are varied to contrast the different sections.

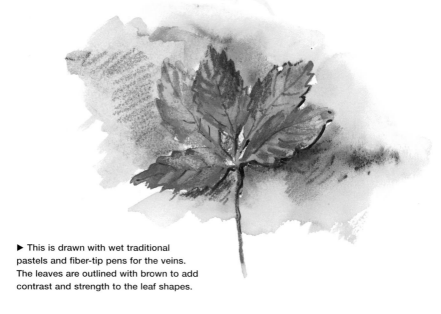

▶ This is drawn with wet traditional pastels and fiber-tip pens for the veins. The leaves are outlined with brown to add contrast and strength to the leaf shapes.

Seasonal trees

Deciduous trees have a basic structure of a trunk, branches, and twigs, which can easily be seen in the winter. This is a very good time to study trees, as well as to sketch lots of them in order to learn how they grow. When you do this, look hard at the tree that you are sketching and don't generalize. Explore how the branches connect to the trunks and the twigs connect to the branches.

Winter tree

Standing back far enough from a large tree, you can see the whole shape. Every different type of tree has a characteristic shape, so observe them carefully because they vary dramatically. Trees are as individual as people, so it would be wrong to generalize their shapes.

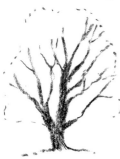

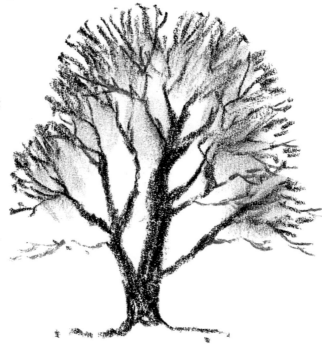

❶ With black conté or charcoal pencil, sketch the trunk and main branches. Close your eyes halfway to simplify the tree's shape and use dots to indicate the outer limits of this shape.

❷ Tiny strokes around the outer edge will suggest a mass of twigs, and gently softening this with a finger gives the impression of fullness.

Summer tree

Trees in full foliage can be daunting to tackle—all those leaves—so we have to learn to simplify their shapes, to seek out the main masses or clumps of foliage, and to find a suitable visual shorthand to use.

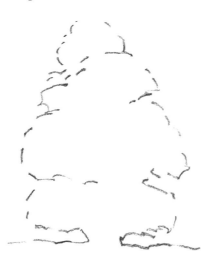

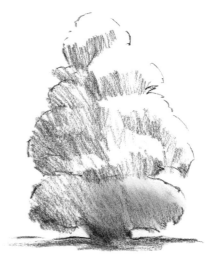

❶ Using a brown pastel pencil, start with the main shape of the tree, making sure that you "plant" the tree in the ground.

❷ Simplify the tree into its main clumps of foliage. Look at the direction of the light— light from the sky and sun will provide shadow areas that you can define with simple parallel lines of shading. Add a shadow on the ground and soften the color gently with a finger.

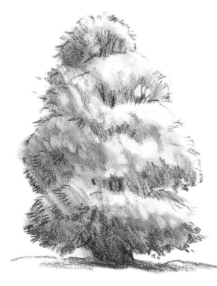

❸ Use a putty eraser to lift out some of the color from the lighter areas, in order to give variations of tone in the foliage. Create some holes in the foliage, so that you can see the sky behind it. With your pencil, deepen the tone of the trunk, add branches in the sky holes and within the foliage, and use tiny dots and strokes to suggest leaves and a filigree edge to the tree.

Seasonal foliage

In a temperate climate the changing seasons bring dramatic changes in the trees, which have a wide range of different colors and textures at different stages throughout the year.

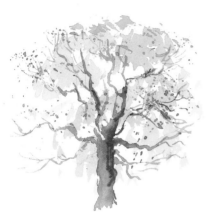

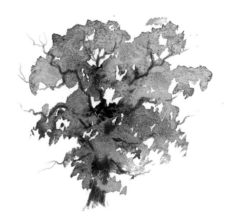

▲ Spring: The tree framework is painted in over a brief sketch, lightening the branches and thinning them out with watery Raw Umber watercolor. Leaf Green is used for the leaves, and the color is splattered on to show the fresh, young foliage.

▲ Summer: The main trunk and some of the branches are drawn in sepia watersoluble pencil. The foliage is painted in Olive Green and Cobalt Blue watercolors, with salt painted on while still wet. When the paint has dried, this is brushed off, and the remaining branches are drawn with pencil.

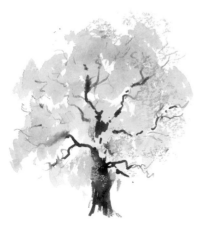

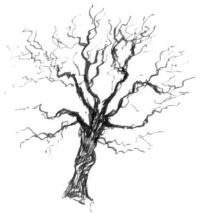

▲ Fall: Orange and yellow washes are used over a framework of Raw Umber paint and pencils, leaving spaces for the bright foliage. When it is dry, add orange oil pastel. Keep some sky holes in the foliage.

▲ Winter: The skeletal shape is exposed. This time of year makes it easier to study the basic structure of a tree. Use a sketch of the sky shapes first to help with the whole effect. This is drawn with a sepia art pen.

EXERCISE ## Paint a fall tree

Try copying this fall tree, which uses salt for the foliage effect. Then find a similar one to try for yourself. Remember not to overwork your trees: you only need to give an impression of the mass of foliage.

The palette Watercolors   Waterproof pen

Neutral   Cerulean   Cadmium   Cadmium   burnt   violet   sepia
Gray   Orange   Yellow   sienna

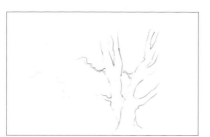

❶ Use a 2B pencil to establish the main shapes, making a note of any spaces between the branches (these add character) and comparing the length of the branches with the trunk to get the proportions correct.

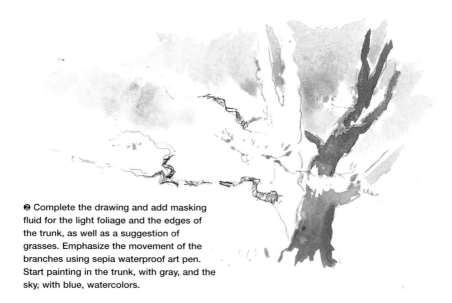

❷ Complete the drawing and add masking fluid for the light foliage and the edges of the trunk, as well as a suggestion of grasses. Emphasize the movement of the branches using sepia waterproof art pen. Start painting in the trunk, with gray, and the sky; with blue, watercolors.

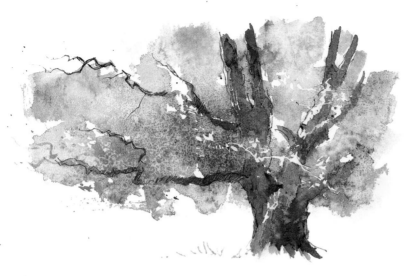

❸ Complete the trunk and add more branches using ink. Dampen the paper over the foliage area, apply a very watery wash of orange, yellow, and brown, then sprinkle with table salt. When it is completely dry, rub off the salt and masking fluid.

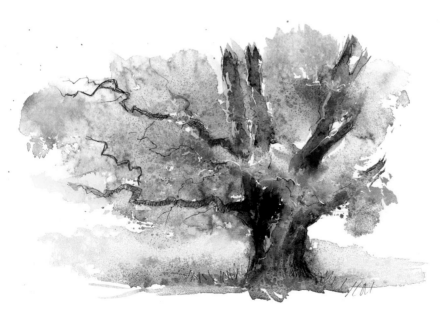

❹ Paint in the base of the tree trunk with brown, and then darken the trunk using Violet. Add in the detail of more branches, this time using ink, and then gently soften the light areas of masking fluid with some pale yellow watercolor.

EXERCISE   Sketch a tree in conté crayon

The simple image of a tree with a rickety fence, makes an ideal subject for sketching. The tree is the important part—the fence is a fun extra.

The palette
Conté crayon

light pressure   medium pressure   firm pressure

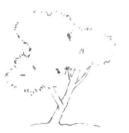

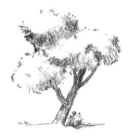

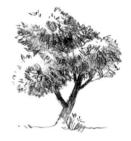

❶ Using black conté, first establish the main shape of the tree, as well as any branches that can be seen through gaps in the foliage. Look closely to discover the direction of the light and see if it reveals the main, large clumps of foliage.

❷ Block in the dark sides of the foliage with the side of the crayon. Carry the dark tone down onto the trunk. The tree will cast a shadow on the trunk; it is darker under the foliage than it is at its base. Suggest grasses with little strokes and dots.

❸ Find a shorthand for the leaves on the tree. Here, mostly short strokes or little V-shapes have been used, with an occasional oval-shape. If you feel tentative, try out some marks on a spare sheet of paper before working on your tree.

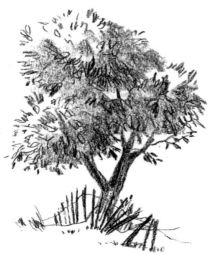

❹ Add in some leaf shapes, particularly around the edges of the tree. Look at mine on the right and in the space in the fork of the tree. Actual leaf shapes will help give the tree character and the drawing credibility. Finally, you can draw in the rickety fence. This is easy and fun—just a few straight lines at different angles, joined by a fine line.

Different trees

Trees present many different faces—bare branches, blossom, full leaf—and they are always an interesting picture to capture. Keep things simple and see how individual trees vary, sometimes dramatically, in color, tone, and texture.

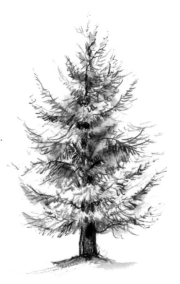

▲ Here, blue and green watersoluble pencils with watersoluble sepia ink are feathered into graceful tapering shapes to create the upward flowing foliage of a conifer.

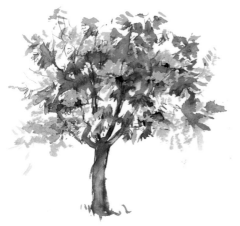

▲ This tree in blossom is painted using dabs of pink oil pastel for the blossoms, which act as a resist to the green and burnt sienna ink and watercolors in the leaves and branches.

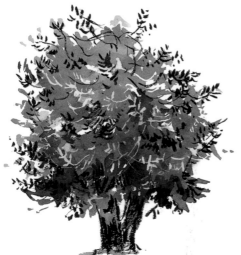

▲ The dense, spiky foliage of black ink and the contrast of masking fluid details against the light green and Cerulean watercolor washes to create this holly tree.

want to know more?

Take it to the next level . . .

Go to . . .
▶ sketch a lake scene—page 132
▶ planning landscapes—page 138

Other sources
▶ **Photographs**
   useful sources of reference
▶ **Art shows**
   look out for local or national events
▶ **Sketchbooks**
   to record different tree shapes
▶ **Horticultural publications**
   for photographs and information on trees
▶ **Publications**
   visit www.harpercollins.com for HarperCollins art books

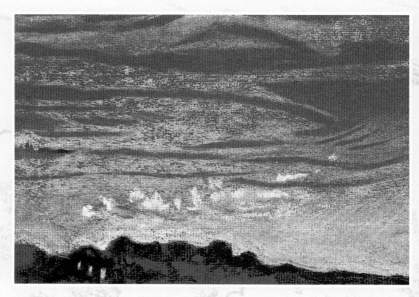

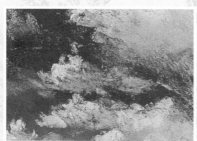
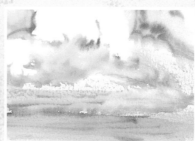

skies

The sky can be the subject of an image, or it can support the rest of your drawing, always providing light, atmosphere, and drama. The blue of the sky is both transparent and weightless, and you need to achieve a suggestion of three dimensions. Cloud formations vary dramatically, and they are always moving, so they require close observation.

Sketching skies

When you are working outdoors, the wind will blow things around, shadows will move, and light will change. You will have to learn how to work quickly. If you like the idea of some practice before embarking on this adventure, try sketching skies through a window. This will teach you how to work quickly, because clouds can change shape within seconds. It helps to know the many different types of clouds—but for the beginner, it's best just to look hard and sketch what you see. Try using different media until you find one that works for you, and the subject, the best.

Clouds in pencil

For sketching clouds, use your softest pencil—a 4B or even a 6B—that gives marks that are easier to erase than hard pencil lines.

❶ Quickly indicate the outline of the largest cloud that you can see, pressing lightly and leaving gaps.

❷ Assess where the light is coming from. Then, using the side of the lead, add some simplified shading to give the cloud its 3-D form. You should try not to make your shapes too monotonously "lumpy" or hard-edged—clouds are soft and wispy. Lift edges that are too hard, or overworked areas, with a putty eraser.

Stormy clouds in charcoal

Charcoal is an excellent medium for sketching storm clouds and skies. You can "move it around" with your fingers and build up layers, or you can use it on its side to create the soft edges that are characteristic of clouds.

❶ Strictly speaking, you do not need to begin with an outline, but if you feel that you need one, start lightly with the sharp point of the charcoal. Soften the marks with your finger if you would like.

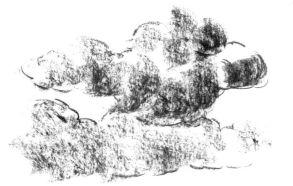

❷ Switch to the side of the charcoal, using a relatively short piece, around 2 inches (5 cm) long. Twist your wrist as you work to suggest the curved undersides of the clouds in places, as shown here with the closest cloud.

❸ Pressing harder with the charcoal still on its side, build up the layers of charcoal to suggest ominous black clouds. Soften some of the top edges with your finger and sweep the charcoal across the paper to create the horizontal bases of the clouds. Finally, suggest some smaller clouds toward the horizon.

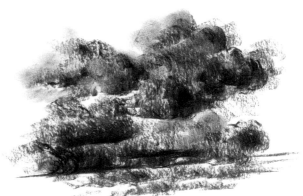

Sketching with watersoluble pencils

Here, just three watersoluble pencils are used for the sky and the cloud; blue-violet, cobalt blue, and turquoise-green, plus some clean water. Work on thick watercolor paper, because it will not buckle when water is added.

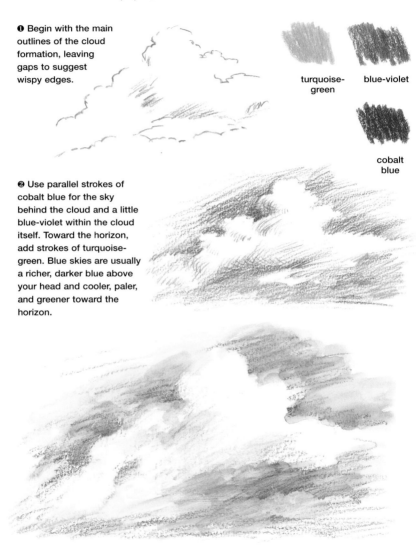

❶ Begin with the main outlines of the cloud formation, leaving gaps to suggest wispy edges.

turquoise-green

blue-violet

cobalt blue

❷ Use parallel strokes of cobalt blue for the sky behind the cloud and a little blue-violet within the cloud itself. Toward the horizon, add strokes of turquoise-green. Blue skies are usually a richer, darker blue above your head and cooler, paler, and greener toward the horizon.

❸ As a sketch, it was complete enough at the last stage, but if you would like to exploit the watersoluble pencils to their full, loosen the color with a brush and clean water. If you use plenty of water, the color will float around, and most of the lines will disappear. Any remaining lines give the impression of a clear blue sky.

Creating color effects

Skies and clouds aren't always blue and white. Different times of the day and different types of weather can create wonderful colors. For this warmer dusk sky, two very different types of materials are used. Never be afraid to mix your materials—anything goes in order to achieve the desired effect.

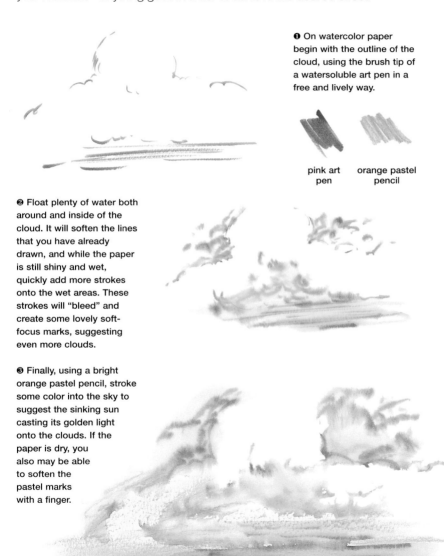

❶ On watercolor paper begin with the outline of the cloud, using the brush tip of a watersoluble art pen in a free and lively way.

pink art pen

orange pastel pencil

❷ Float plenty of water both around and inside of the cloud. It will soften the lines that you have already drawn, and while the paper is still shiny and wet, quickly add more strokes onto the wet areas. These strokes will "bleed" and create some lovely soft-focus marks, suggesting even more clouds.

❸ Finally, using a bright orange pastel pencil, stroke some color into the sky to suggest the sinking sun casting its golden light onto the clouds. If the paper is dry, you also may be able to soften the pastel marks with a finger.

A sky sketchbook

A sky is constantly changing, so you are free to depict it in abstract shapes without the fear of your sketches being considered "wrong." Keeping a sky sketchbook will help you handle pastels with confidence. Produce one study per day and make a note of the time and date.

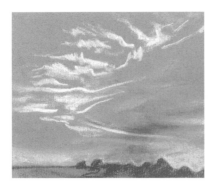

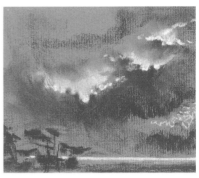

▲ This is one of a set of studies made early each morning from my bedroom window, using white and gray pastels and a sketchbook with paper of assorted colors.

▲ Make a study at the same time for three weeks. Select paper of a color that matches the general tone of the sky and use white for highlights and gray for darker tones.

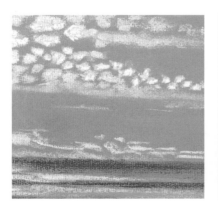

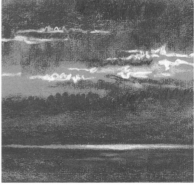

▲ After a few days, add a colored pastel to the white and the gray. Lay the broadest bands of pastel first, finishing with the smaller details. Here pale blue was followed by gray and then by white. While it is not a strict rule, it is usually more effective to leave the white until the end.

▲ In this sketch gray was applied first, leaving a thin line at the horizon. This was followed by blue, yellow, and white. You will not find dramatic effects in the sky every day, but low cloud cover will give you some practice of blending even tones on paper.

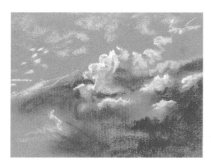

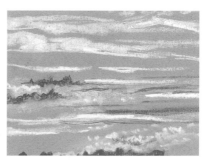

▲ Try making sky studies while you are moving—watching from the windows of a train offers an excellent opportunity. Here, white was applied before gray. They were blended together before further accents of white were added to the tops of the clouds.

▲ If you are tempted to record architectural or landscape features, keep them simple and just add some written notes, otherwise you will become lost in the details. Dawn and dusk are good times for sky studies since the land is mostly lost in the dim light.

▶ When you return home from a journey, play with your studies. Experiment with reproducing the sketches using the same pastels but on papers of different tones and colors. You will find that you are able to change the mood of the subject.

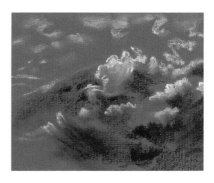

▼ Changing the background will also encourage you to explore different methods of creating the effects that you want. Here, on dark-toned paper streaks are lifted with an eraser instead of being drawn directly.

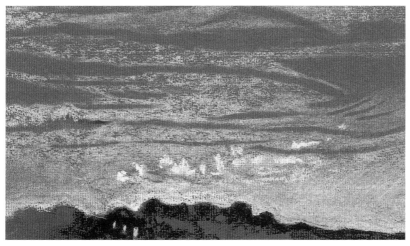

EXERCISE | Clouds in charcoal and conté

You can choose a simple combination of black and white on a warm-colored background for a dramatic and effective sketch—proof that you don't always have to use blue for sky! Experiment with some different colored backgrounds to produce varying effects.

The palette
Conté crayon

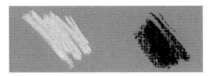

white conté crayon   charcoal

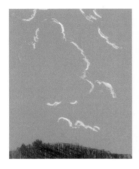

❶ On colored paper—or white paper stained with a used tea bag—use the side of a piece of charcoal to suggest a hillside with a few trees. Then position the clouds with the point of a white conté stick or a white pastel pencil.

❷ Using the side of the charcoal again, block in the darker parts of the clouds, to suggest their fullness. Use curving strokes to emphasize the form of the clouds.

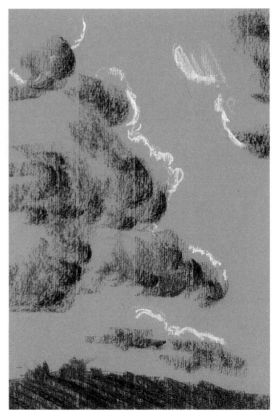

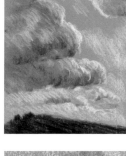

❸ Smooth some of the charcoal marks into the paper with a finger. You can then begin to sketch in the lighter parts of the clouds with white, using some curving linear strokes and following the form of the clouds. Use simple side strokes for the wispy clouds against the sky.

❹ Build up the forms of the clouds, using charcoal for the bottoms of the clouds and marks in white for the cloud tops and the details. Where the white mixes with the charcoal, it forms a useful soft gray, which adds to the feeling of fullness. Press hard with the white crayon for sharply lit edges. Spray with fixative.

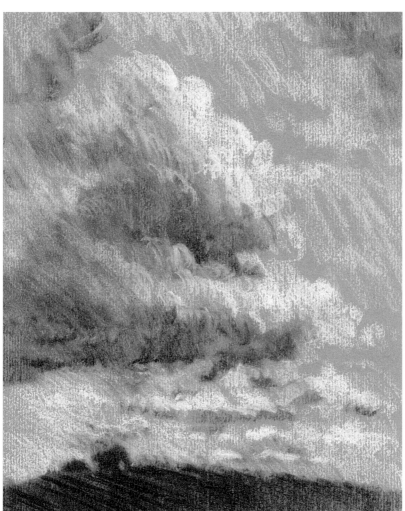

EXERCISE   Billowing clouds in pastels

Only six pastel sticks were used for this scene, which captures the fluffiness
of clouds and the blue bowl of the sky. Notice how the clouds diminish in
size as they get close to the horizon—this gives a feeling of space.

The palette
Pastels

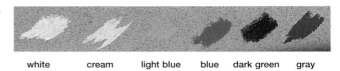

white   cream   light blue   blue   dark green   gray

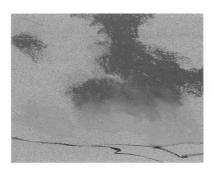

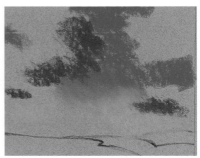

❶ Using the point of a dark green pastel,
suggest the land. Using the sides of the
pastels, block in the blue sky shapes, leaving
spaces for the clouds. Blue sky is always
cooler and lighter close to the horizon.
Blend the two blues together with a finger,
where they meet.

❷ Using a gray pastel, block in the darker
sides of the clouds, to show their three-
dimensional form. You could also use
purple-gray, or even gray-green, for this
step—clouds are more interesting with a
variety of colors in their depths.

❸ Using a cream pastel and a light touch,
stroke cream over the empty spaces, as
well as the gray, to create the main areas of
fluffy clouds. Vary your pressure; a light
touch will provide feathery edges. Gently
blend with a finger in places. Stroke the
side of the green pastel over the landscape.

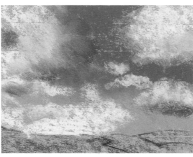

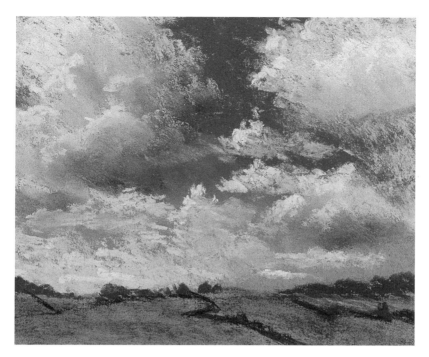

❹ Add more cream pastel, pressing hard for more solid areas in the mass of clouds, and stroking gently to create the feathery cloud edges. Using the tip of a white pastel, press hard to define the sunlit edges of the clouds. Finally, add some tiny clouds close to the horizon and, using the dark gray pastel, add trees and shrubs to the landscape and gently blend the green with a finger for a textured look.

MUST KNOW

Creating mood

Skies and cloud formations change constantly, and what you choose to draw and how, will affect the mood of your sketch. You can opt for soft, subtle early morning skies, dramatic light effects with towering dark storm clouds and rain, or a gentle sunrise or sunset, which means that you can have fun with colored pencils or pastels.

want to know **more?**

Take it to the next level . . .

Go to . . .

▶ sketching water—page 128
▶ planning landscapes—page 138
▶ a walk along the beach in pastels—
   page 182

Other sources
▶ **Photographs**
   useful sources of reference
▶ **Art shows**
   look out for local or national events
▶ **Art galleries**
   study how the old masters drew skies
▶ **Painting vacations**
   expand your horizons with other artists
▶ **Publications**
   visit www.harpercollins.com for
   HarperCollins art books

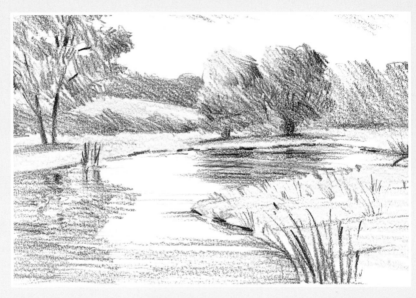

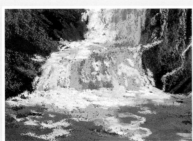

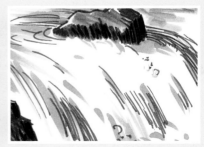

water

Water often reflects both the sky and the land, and reflections are transformed into fascinating abstract shapes by ripples and movement. Depicting water presents the artist with a lot of variety—whether it's still water, moving or falling water, clear or muddy water, waves, ripples, or reflections. Water is able to provide us with inexhaustible diversity.

▶ Sketching water

Since water is intrinsically transparent, we are actually
sketching surface reflections, instead of the water itself.
These reflections are constantly in motion—even in
apparently still water—so we have to try our best to capture
this movement. Once again, closing your eyes halfway will
help you simplify what you see, and this is very important;
you do not need to capture every ripple or eddy.

Still water

Begin these simple exercises with a stick of charcoal, choosing a fat piece
that can easily be used on its side.

❶ Using the side of a piece
of charcoal, make a few
overlapping vertical strokes.
To match the bottom half of
the illustration, blend these
strokes with a finger.

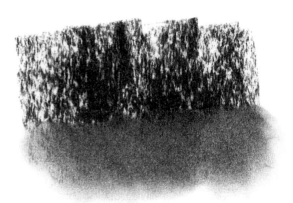

❷ Now for the magic part.
Break off a small piece of
putty eraser and mold it into
a point with your fingers.
Stroke it horizontally across
the charcoal, to give the
impression of gentle
movement to the surface of
the water. As you look
across an expanse of water,
these marks will gradually
close up, giving the
suggestion of space.

Reflections in calm water

Objects that are reflected in calm water can appear to be mirror images, but there are some slight differences that you need to observe carefully. Dark objects are always slightly lighter; light objects (including the sky) are slightly darker. Tiny ripples will break up the reflections, leaving gaps.

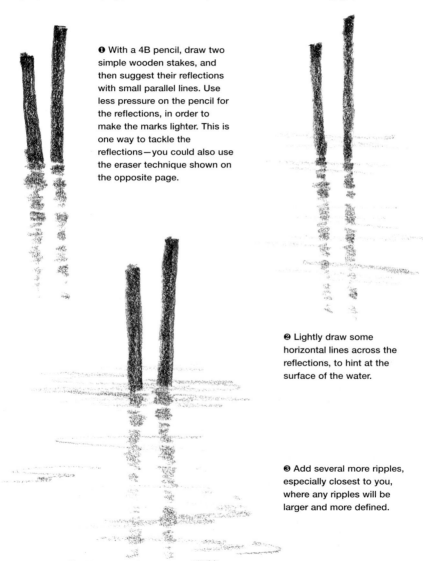

❶ With a 4B pencil, draw two simple wooden stakes, and then suggest their reflections with small parallel lines. Use less pressure on the pencil for the reflections, in order to make the marks lighter. This is one way to tackle the reflections—you could also use the eraser technique shown on the opposite page.

❷ Lightly draw some horizontal lines across the reflections, to hint at the surface of the water.

❸ Add several more ripples, especially closest to you, where any ripples will be larger and more defined.

Moving water

Wind will disturb the surface of pond and lake water, creating waves, and water will create patterns as it moves along. Rocks in the path of moving water will force the water to swirl around them. Before sketching moving water, spend time just watching and analyzing what you see.

❶ Using a pale turquoise and a bright blue pencil, draw a series of shallow, curved lines, allowing some of them to meet in little, inverted V-shapes to suggest the tops of the waves.

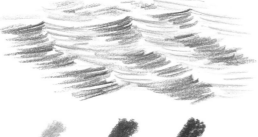

pale turquoise   bright blue   dark green

❷ Now sketch in the right-hand sides of the waves, using firm strokes of blue and dark green. Leave the paler color to suggest light on the surface from the left. Make the waves that are close to you bigger.

❶ Using a conté pencil, begin by drawing a chunky rock, using small, vertical strokes to suggest its surface. Place a few tiny, horizontal curving lines for the moving water.

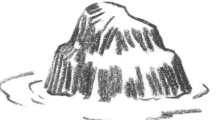

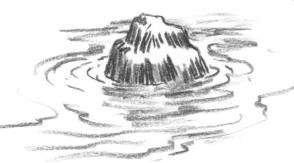

❷ Build up the ripples around the rock, using close lines underneath the rock to suggest a broken reflection. Flick the lines onto the paper with swift movements of the pencil; do not work too hard on the strokes, otherwise you will lose the sense of movement.

Waterfall

To capture the sight of water rushing over a waterfall, the white of the paper can be left to be read as foam. An alternative approach would be to work on a colored background, using white conté or pastel pencil, for the foam.

❶ Using a red-brown art pen, draw a rock and suggest more rocks on the riverbank with vertical strokes and some crosshatching. Then, using the soft brush tip of a pale turquoise pastel, begin to suggest the moving water, curving some of your marks down the page.

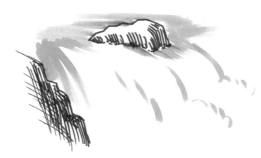

red-brown pale turquoise dark green

❷ Build up more curving marks for the rushing water, along with smaller curves for the bubbles and foam at the base. Now add a few strokes of pale turquoise over the rocks too.

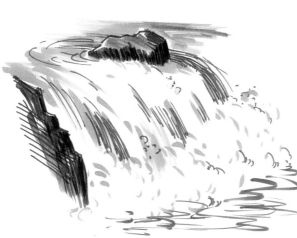

❸ Using the pen end of a dark green art pen, emphasize the rushing nature of the water using curving strokes around the rock and down into the foam. Use some tiny dots, and arcs in the foam, and finally, swiftly sketch in some lines at the base of the foam with the brush tip to show fast-moving water.

EXERCISE # A lake scene in colored pencils

Only four colored pencils were used for this simple lake scene, which is an opportunity to practice sketching trees and water. Try a similar sketch from life for yourself: just four pencils and some paper are easy to carry!

The palette
Colored pencils

| gold-yellow | cobalt blue | bottlegreen | dark blue |

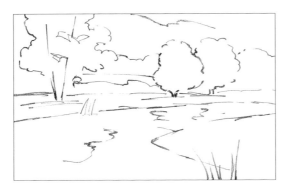

❶ With an HB pencil, lightly sketch in the main elements. Lift up the pencil marks slightly with a putty eraser once you are happy with the composition.

❷ Begin with the lightest color, gold-yellow, and using parallel shading strokes, work across the trees, bank, and land. Begin to add bottlegreen.

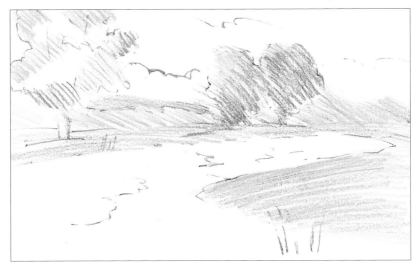

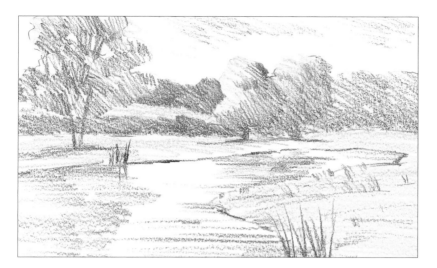

❸ Use bottlegreen for the bushes and the trees, the reeds by the water, and the trees' shadows. Press hard here and there to emphasize the bank of the lake and draw parallel, horizontal lines in the water to suggest the trees' reflections. Use cobalt blue for the sky and horizontal lines on the water, reflecting the sky.

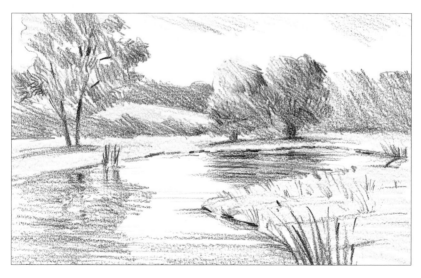

❹ Using dark blue and short, linear strokes, darken the sides of the trees that are in shadow on the right, the trunk, and the branches of the left-hand tree, and then darken the tree reflections in the water. Short strokes will emphasize the near bank and bring it forward. Finally, add a few dark reeds to finish the picture.

EXERCISE # Sketch a waterfall in pastels

A tumbling waterfall is an appealing subject, and this one creates a lovely shape on the paper. Always squint at your subject—it simplifies the shapes.

The palette

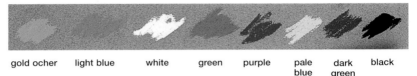

gold ocher   light blue   white   green   purple   pale blue   dark green   black

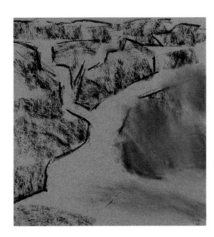

❶ You can create an arrangement of almost abstract shapes on the paper, using charcoal to define the rock areas and leaving the paper untouched for the water area. Block in the shapes with the charcoal, and then smudge a little with a tissue to soften any hard lines and blend the charcoal, as shown on the right side of the picture.

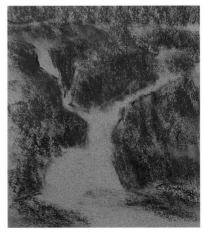

❷ With your darkest pastels, loosely block in the colors, using the side of the pastel. The colors can be placed in a relatively random way, since you are simply creating an "underpainting." Blend the colors in places with a finger and leave other areas unblended to suggest texture.

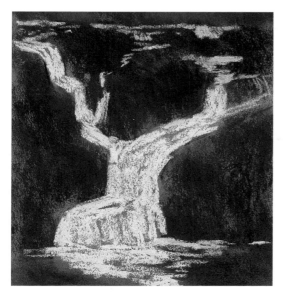

❸ Add in some dark, rich purple to give some warmth and variety to the rocks, and then, using pale blue, use directional strokes for the water, following its path. If you look closely at the passages of water, you will be able to see the direction of the strokes.

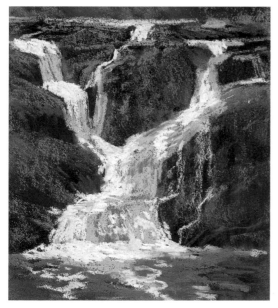

❹ Suggest sunlight on the rocks with a gold ocher pastel; the sunlight on the water is created with white. Add medium blue linear strokes to the water at the foot of the waterfall. Lightly "scumble" touches of all the medium tones lightly over the rocks to suggest lichen and texture.

want to know more?

Take it to the next level . . .

Go to . . .
▶ **Seaside sketching**—page 178
▶ **A walk along the beach in pastel**— page 182
▶ **Seascape in watercolor**—page 186

Other sources
▶ **Photographs**
   useful sources of reference
▶ **Art shows**
   look at subjects and composition
▶ **Trips to the seaside or country**
   sketch any water subjects you see
▶ **Painting vacations**
   expand your horizons with other artists
▶ **Publications**
   visit www.harpercollins.com for HarperCollins art books

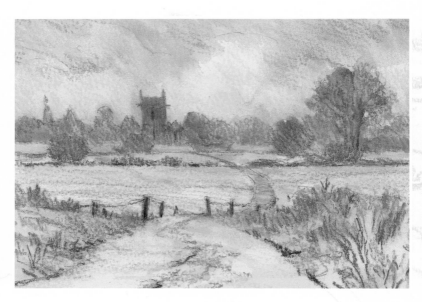

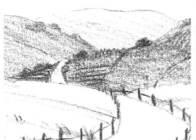

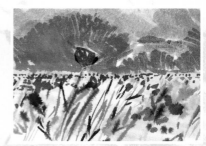

landscapes

A good landscape requires
the mastery of many elements:
drawing, tone, color, texture,
form, space, and atmosphere.
If you are going to become a
good landscape artist, you
need to be prepared to spend
some of your time outdoors
sketching. You will experience
a wide range of changing light
effects as well as the sheer
joy and exhilaration of drawing
and sketching.

Planning landscapes

**In general, when you are tackling a landscape, it's a good
idea to consider three main areas—foreground, middle
distance, and distance. If you handle these areas successfully,
the viewer's eye will move back through the picture, as if they
are walking through the landscape into the distance beyond.**

Distance

To achieve a real sense of depth in a landscape sketch, you will need to
consider two things. First, the farther away, the paler things will become.
This is called "atmospheric perspective." Second, the farther away they are,
the smaller things will become. This is an oversimplification, but you will be
successful if you observe, measure, and try to faithfully reproduce tones.
It will teach you a great deal if you work in monochrome to begin with.

▶ This pencil sketch of a mountain range
shows how distance is implied by very pale
tones farthest away and strongest tones in
the foreground. Atmospheric perspective
interferes with vision, making tones lighter,
less contrasting, and bluer, which is why
distant trees, hills, and buildings appear to
be similar in tone and somewhat blue.

▼ This pencil sketch clearly shows that
objects that are close to you appear to be
much larger than those that are far away.
The rocks and grasses are much bigger than

the trees in the distance, and yet we know,
intellectually, that this cannot be the case.
Always measure in order to double-check
the sizes of objects in a landscape picture.

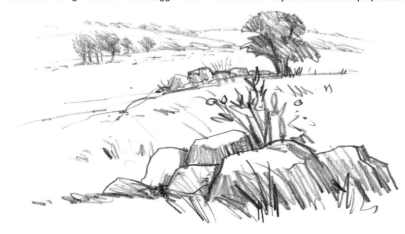

Creating depth

This little example shows you how to create a sense of depth in a sketch. Use a colored pencil—any color will work. If you decide to work from a photo of your own, be careful—sometimes photos fail to capture the subtle tones in the distance. Lighten the distance if you need to.

❶ Begin with the main outlines in the landscape, measuring the sizes of the shapes that you can see. Landscape will constantly surprise you; distant fields are often much smaller than you would expect. Try to make use of overlapping forms like these, they help suggest space.

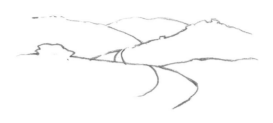

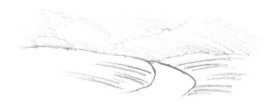

❷ Lightly add shading over all of the distant hills, using the same tone throughout. Use a few parallel lines in the foreground.

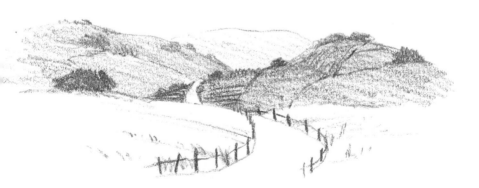

❸ Build up the tone of the second and third hills gradually, increasing the strength of the tone. Finally, draw in the details on the landscape, ensuring that the trees are larger on the closer hill and smaller farther away. Flick in some tiny grasses in the foreground. Notice that these marks are bigger than the distant trees.

Foreground

If your sketch is going to include foreground, middle distance, and far distance, then a very busy foreground may prevent the eye from moving back into the picture. The problem is that the foreground will dominate our vision because it is so close to us, and the temptation to include too much is very strong. We have to learn to use what we see very selectively. Here are a few clues for the successful use of foreground features.

▶ Putting roads, pathways, and riverbanks in the foreground will lead the eye of the viewer from the edge of the picture into the middle or far distance.

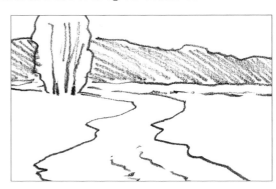

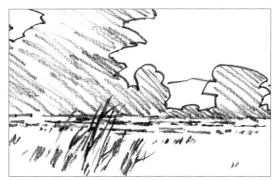

◀ If there is not an obvious path or edge to lead us in, we can use marks to suggest the surface of the ground. Here, grasses, some of which are tall enough to link the foreground and the background, have been used, but on a beach, for instance, it could be piles of sand or pebbles. If it was water, it could be ripples.

▶ Shadows can be very useful in a picture: here, they break up a flat foreground area and lead the viewer's eye back to the trees.

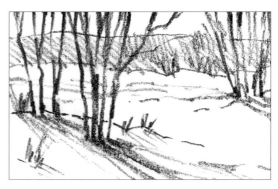

❶ Using a colored pencil, begin with the main, large landscape elements in the distance, leaving space at the base for the foreground. Tiny, parallel strokes depict grass in the middle distance.

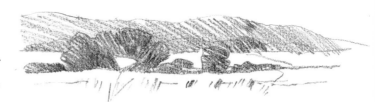

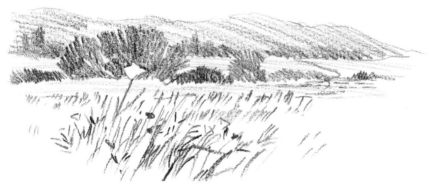

❷ Remember, the closer to you, the bigger the objects—here, the grasses and wild flowers are taller than the distant trees. Use parallel strokes, dots, and dashes for the grasses and little zigzag shapes for leaves and petals. In the foreground the contrasts are strongest. Press hard so that dark marks strongly contrast against the white paper.

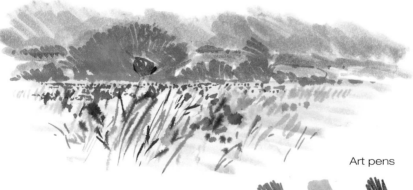

▲ For this sketch, art pens are used. Begin with the distance, keeping colors light, then stroke pale green over the ground and dissolve it with water. While the paper is still damp, add the foreground grasses and flowers and, on the wet paper, some of the lines became fuzzy, which is perfect for sketching leaves and flowers.

Art pens

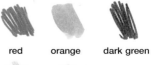

red   orange   dark green

pale blue   pale green   turquoise

EXERCISE Middle distance in mixed media

This little sketch, which is only 7 x 9 inches (18 x 23 cm), was created relatively quickly, using watersoluble felt-tip pens and just a few soft pastels. Like most garden scenes, it shows both the foreground and the middle distance.

The palette Watersoluble felt-tip pens

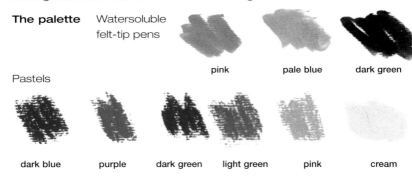

pink   pale blue   dark green

Pastels

dark blue   purple   dark green   light green   pink   cream

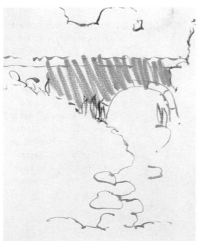

❶ With a pink watersoluble felt-tip pen, sketch in the outline of the bridge and the dry streambed. Suggest some foliage and the trees behind with a blue felt-tip pen. Begin to loosely block in the color shapes.

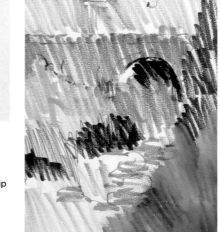

❷ Continue to block in colors, bringing in some darker areas with a dark green felt-tip pen. When all the shapes are blocked in, begin to dissolve the marks with a wet paintbrush and some clear water. Do not worry if the colors run into each other.

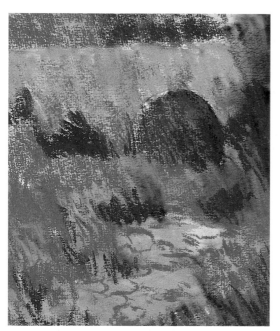

❸ Allow the sheet to dry, and then, using a pink pastel, a purple, a dark blue, and two different greens, work over the watercolor base, using both side strokes and linear marks to suggest foliage.

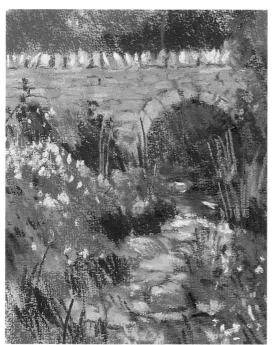

❹ Now bring in the lightest cream pastel and, with some linear dots and dashes, add tiny wild flowers; lighten the top of the bridge and some of the stones in the fore-ground, and then use the point of the purple pastel to carefully pick out small, dark details. Build up the foliage area and add long, linear strokes, both dark and light, to suggest the tall grasses and reeds.

EXERCISE Distant landscape in pastels

Distance in a landscape is usually achieved with a change of scale, cooler color, and lighter tones. Often, distant hills are seen to be a glorious blue-purple, their local color filtered and softened by the veils of atmosphere between us and the distance.

The palette
Pastels

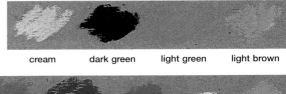

cream   dark green   light green   light brown

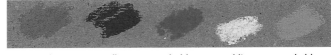

turquoise   medium   purple-blue   white   pale blue
blue-green

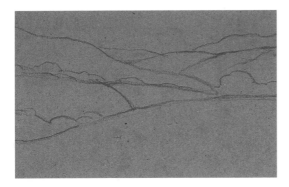

❶ On a soft brown sheet of pastel paper draw in the main shapes of the landscape, using a blue pastel pencil, which will blend well with subsequent applications of color. There is no need for detail at this stage—the main shapes will be sufficient.

❷ Using a relatively light touch, begin to block in color, using the sides of the pastels. Use pale blue and cream for the sky, purple-blue and pale blue for the distant hills, cool medium blue-green for the closer hill and some of the tree shapes, turquoise for the middle distance fields, and a soft light brown for the foreground.

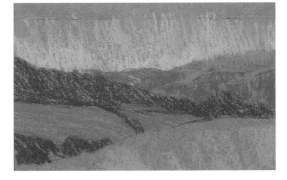

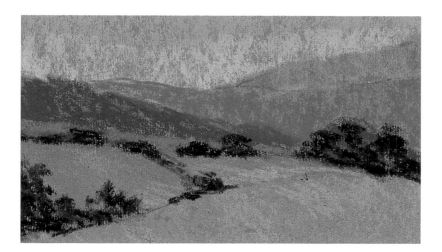

❸ Using the darkest green, use short, linear strokes with the tip of the pastel, to create the trees and hedges, varying the scale and the shapes. Notice how tiny touches for hedges and tiny shapes for fields will emphasize the sense of space in your drawing. Now begin to introduce some long strokes of warm light green into the foreground field, in order to suggest the presence of grasses.

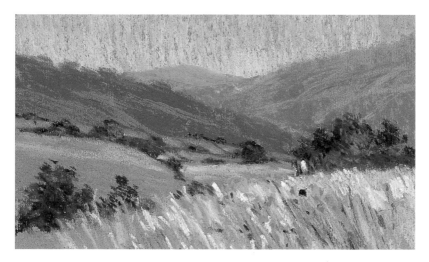

❹ Use tiny touches to describe the trees and vary the tone with subtle touches of medium green to suggest light on the foliage. Use cream and dark green linear strokes for long grasses in the foreground. Stroke lighter tones—cream and green— over the fields in the middle distance, pressing hard for more positive color, and stroke the side of the cream pastel gently over the sky, to create a visual blend. Dots and dashes of both blues in the foreground suggest wild flowers—the finishing touch.

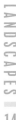

EXERCISE # Landscape in pastel pencils

Often, by copying another artist's work, we can learn a great deal that we can then use at a later date. Do not worry if your colors differ; just work through the steps—you will learn a lot along the way.

The palette

Pastel pencils

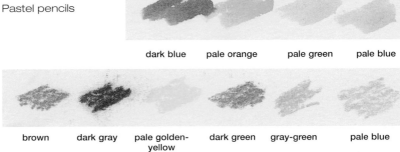

dark blue   pale orange   pale green   pale blue

brown   dark gray   pale golden-yellow   dark green   gray-green   pale blue

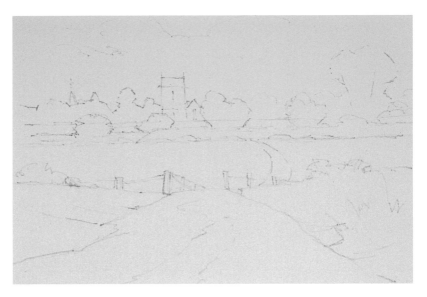

❶ Working on a sheet of cream-colored watercolor paper, you can lightly sketch in the main elements of the landscape, using an HB pencil. You could work directly with the point of an art pen, but you will find that a pencil is easier to correct.

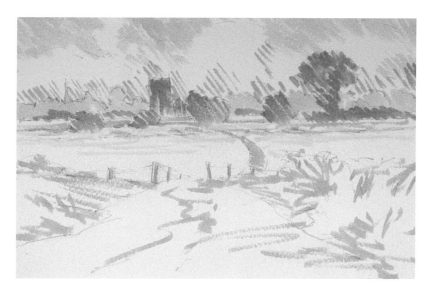

❷ Using the brush tip of a pale blue art pen, roughly block in the sky, distant trees, and a few horizontal lines in the distant field. Using a pale orange art pen, add some lines behind the trees and swiftly suggest the rough foliage in the foreground and the track.

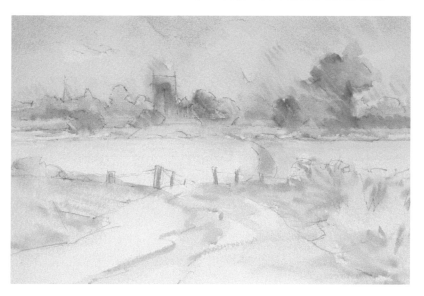

❸ Now dip a brush in some clean water and literally float the water over your picture. You will see that the lines of ink dissolve, leaving you with a lovely atmospheric "underpainting" on which you can finish your sketch.

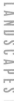

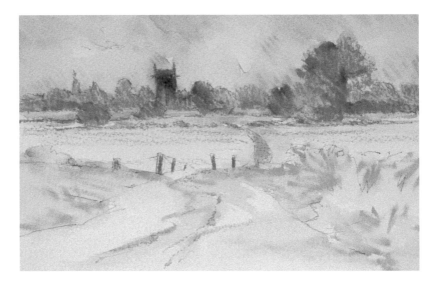

❹ When the picture is completely dry, use small strokes of a pale blue pastel pencil for the distance. Do not press too hard—the texture of the paper will break up the marks. Very lightly stroke a few horizontal lines over the distant field.

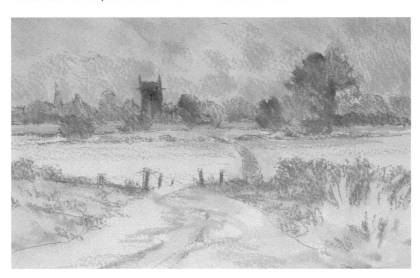

❺ With a pale golden-yellow pastel pencil, work on the clouds behind the church, the ground under the church, and in front of the distant trees. With a soft gray-green, suggest the foreground hedgerow and grasses with little scribbles.

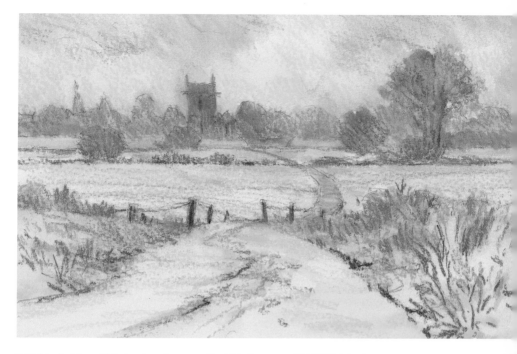

⑤ Finished picture: Tinted watercolor paper, 7 x 10 inches (18 x 25 cm). Finishing the picture is enjoyable, but it is easy to overdo final touches. Using a dark green, define the hedgerow with small, flicked marks. Switch to brown and add more grasses, then go over some of the closer trees and shrubs. Soften the color in the clouds with more pale golden-yellow and use this color on the road, both in the foreground and in the middle distance. Finally, with dark gray, sharpen up a few foreground details—in the road and on the fence posts. Stop if you think that you are adding too much.

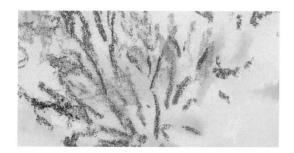

Detail: This area of the picture shows how well the strokes of pastel work over the art pen brushstrokes.

want to know **more?**

Take it to the next level . . .

Go to . . .
▶ **sketching water**—page 128
▶ **sketch a street scene**—page 172
▶ **seaside sketching**—page 178

Other sources
▶ **Photographs**
  useful sources of reference
▶ **Art galleries**
  look at others painters' work
▶ **Sketchbooks**
  keep a record of what you see
▶ **Painting vacations**
  expand your horizons with other artists
▶ **Publications**
  visit www.harpercollins.com for HarperCollins art books

people and

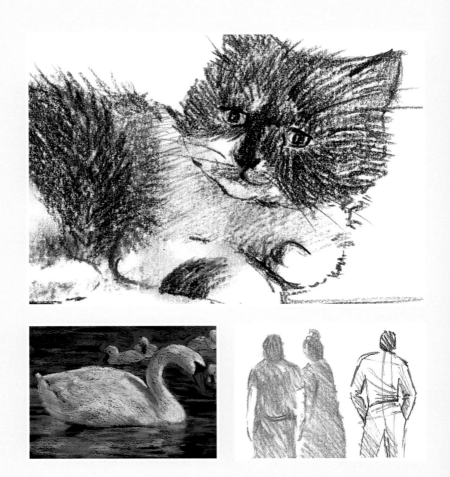

animals

The human figure has inspired artists ever since man began to paint on cave walls. The appeal of the human form is limitless— no matter how small a figure is in a scene, it will attract attention before any other element. Animals can also add a touch of life to a sketch, and many artists find them to be very engaging and rewarding subjects in their own right.

Sketching people

Figures can make or mar a picture. You may be able to distort a tree slightly and get away with it, but a distorted figure will just look wrong. This section is about ways to draw figures quickly and convincingly, so that you can include them in your sketches. Carry a pocket sketchbook and practice whenever you can—in the library, while you wait at a station, in airports or cafés.

Simple figure

When you are drawing a single figure, you may have time to concentrate on the proportions. If these are right, the figure will look convincing. In a quick sketch don't worry about details such as hands or feet—go for the shape.

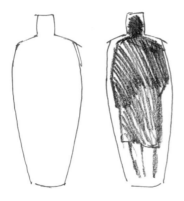

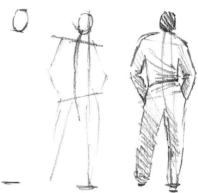

▲ Pretend that your figure isn't human and draw it how you would draw a bottle, thinking about the shape and the outline. The head becomes the stopper on the bottle, and the arms and legs become part of the body of the bottle.

▲ If the figure is leaning, draw the head and a line for the feet. Draw a line from the head down through the body, to show the direction of the spine. Add lines for the shoulders and hips, looking at the angle.

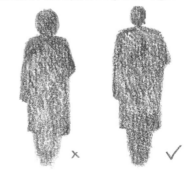

▶ Make the heads of your figures smaller than you think that they are. A head that is too large will make your figure look like a tall child or a figure with a balloonlike head.

Multiple figures

Groups of figures present a challenge, but a simple, large shape, with a few carefully placed heads and a few legs, will often give the impression of a group, without you needing to add too many details!

▶ Where two figures are side-by-side, squint to see the shape that they make together and draw that shape. Then add just enough details to show that there are two figures.

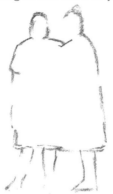

Woman in doorway

This woman is standing by her doorway. Always try to put some of the surroundings into a figure sketch. They will provide scale and a location for your figure. A little sketch like this might be useful for a future painting.

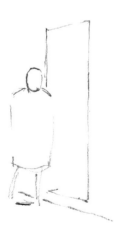 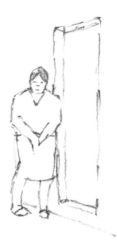 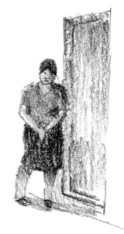

❶ Begin sketching the main shape of the figure in pencil, the stance of the legs if they are in an unusual position, and a few well-constructed lines for the doorway.

❷ Add in more detail—the position of the arms, eyes, nose, and mouth. This isn't strictly necessary, but it is helpful to hint at features if a figure is facing you.

❸ Use colored pencils to complete the sketch: brown for the skirt and the doorway, and also to darken the legs under the skirt. Add a shadow on the ground.

Drawing after Degas

Copying an old master's work is an excellent way to learn—one that is used by many students at art school. One of the dancer drawings by Edgar Degas is recreated here, using only four sticks of conté crayon.

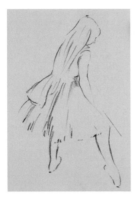

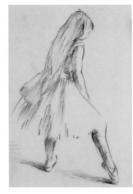

❷ You must study the original drawing carefully and strengthen the line work to include any areas of shadow/tone. Notice how Degas anchored his figure to the ground with the shadows, so that the figure does not float in space. Try to make your lines follow the form—around the arm muscles, down the skirt, hair, and back leg.

❶ Copy the main lines, being very careful with the proportions. If you feel uncertain about your ability to copy accurately, it is acceptable to enlarge the original and then trace the outline, but in your sketch try to keep your line work sensitive: light in places and heavier in the areas of shadow.

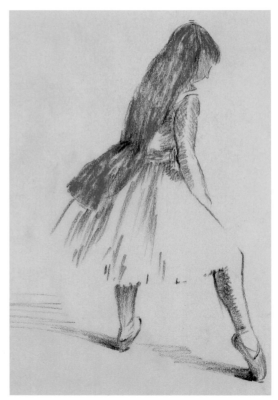

❸ Although the girl in the original drawing had black hair, use some red conté to strongly contrast with the blue bow on the back of the dress. This is a device Degas used often. Gently apply the red conté to the skin but press firmly for the hair. Add strokes of blue to the bow.

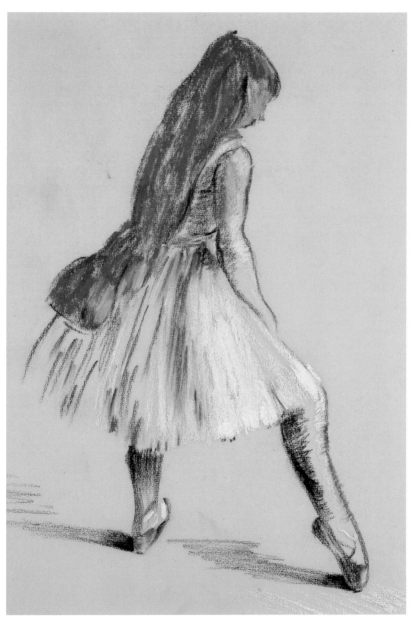

❹ Complete the drawing with white conté. Gently stroke over the red conté, it will give a pink skin tone. Press hard for highlights. Use long, vertical strokes of white for the dress.

Use short, horizontal marks down the front of the leg and add touches of white to the blue bow—it will blend with the blue. Finally, add a few strokes of white on the floor.

Sketching animals

A few sheep or cows in a landscape—or a cat in a garden—
can add life and interest to a scene, so practice sketching
animals whenever you can. Be prepared for the fact that
they always move when you don't want them to—if this
worries you, you can find sleeping creatures to sketch! Use
a big sheet of paper, and if your model moves, sketch another
pose; when it moves again, start another sketch. Fill the sheet
with sketches, and gradually you will learn the animal's shape.

Sheep and cows

Try to simplify the shape of the animal as quickly as possible, perhaps with
a basic geometric shape, and complete as much of the pose as you can.
Even if the animal moves, the chances are that it will return to that pose,
and you can gradually add more details.

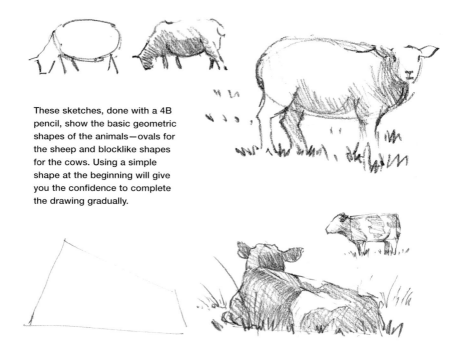

These sketches, done with a 4B
pencil, show the basic geometric
shapes of the animals—ovals for
the sheep and blocklike shapes
for the cows. Using a simple
shape at the beginning will give
you the confidence to complete
the drawing gradually.

Tortoiseshell kitten

When they have finished racing around at top speed, kittens will collapse and sit still for a long time. They are lovely subjects for sketching. When they are tiny, their heads seem to be too big for their little bodies.

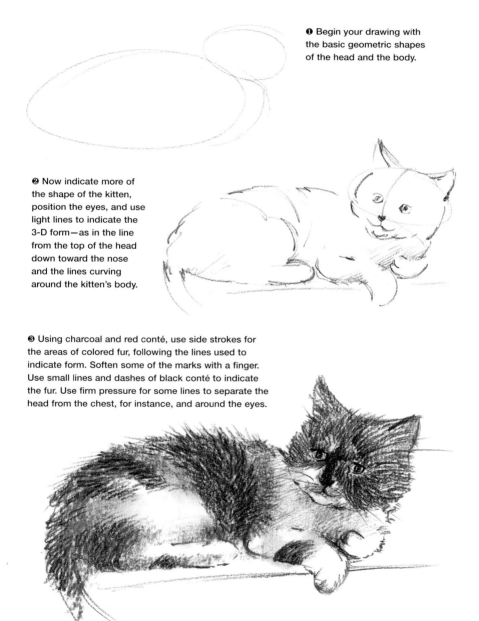

❶ Begin your drawing with the basic geometric shapes of the head and the body.

❷ Now indicate more of the shape of the kitten, position the eyes, and use light lines to indicate the 3-D form—as in the line from the top of the head down toward the nose and the lines curving around the kitten's body.

❸ Using charcoal and red conté, use side strokes for the areas of colored fur, following the lines used to indicate form. Soften some of the marks with a finger. Use small lines and dashes of black conté to indicate the fur. Use firm pressure for some lines to separate the head from the chest, for instance, and around the eyes.

EXERCISE   Swan and cygnets on black paper

Brightly-colored pastel will seem to glow on any dark paper, especially black. You can either use soft pastels or hard sticks, but don't use pastel pencils. Sketching from a photograph is perfectly acceptable, but you should also spend some time sketching birds and animals from life.

The palette Pastels

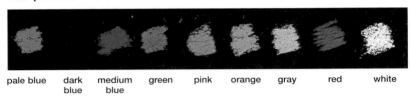

| pale blue | dark blue | medium blue | green | pink | orange | gray | red | white |

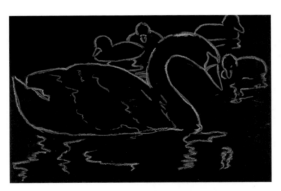

❶ Draw the main outlines of your subject onto the black paper, using a light-colored pastel—pale blue or even white will work. The outline can be hard, since eventually it will be obscured by subsequent layers of pastel.

❷ Roughly block in some of the colors, using medium tones of blue for the swan and purple-pink for the cygnets, with some touches of pale blue on top. This is, in effect, an "underpainting," since you are working from dark to light, and you will layer light tones on top later.

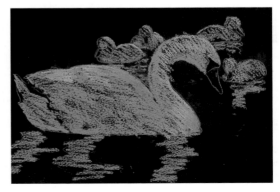

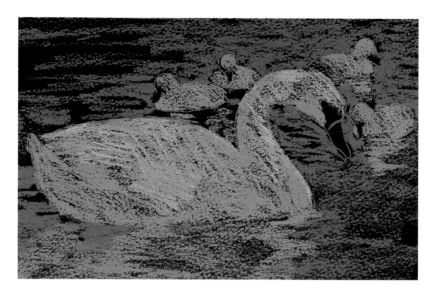

❸ Using a slightly darker blue, suggest the surface of the water with some horizontal strokes. Work on the cygnets, adding some lighter blue to the pink—cygnets are a pinkish-gray color. At this point, you should lightly spray the picture with some fixative. It will help keep the lighter layers from mixing with the darker ones.

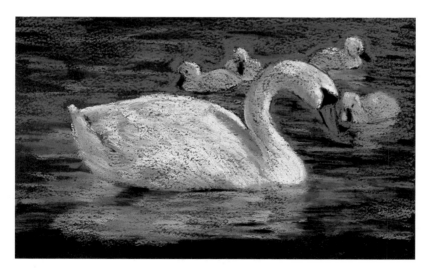

❹ Now you can enjoy adding the lighter tones, mixing color by building one color over another with small crosshatched lines to achieve the tone that you want. The cygnets, for example, are a mixture of pink, blue, and tiny touches of orange. The head of the swan is touched with orange, and there are pinks and blues in the shadows and white for the sunlit feathers. Finally, add dark blue and touches of green to the water.

EXERCISE   Sketch a boy and his dog

Since both people and animals move around so much, try to develop "speed sketches," capturing main shapes and not including unnecessary details. If you copy this exercise or work from a photo, set a timer for around five minutes maximum, and try to work much faster than usual. This will force you to simplify.

The palette
3B pencil

light tone

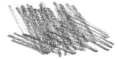

medium tone

dark tone

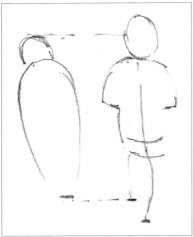

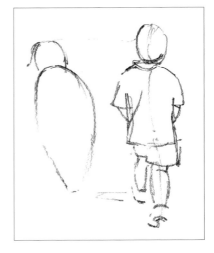

❶ Using a 3B pencil, start your drawing by quickly capturing the main shapes of your subject. Before continuing, carefully check the proportions. You can see that this little boy's head fits into his body four times (most adults are around seven "heads" high). Unlike adults, children's heads are relatively big in relation to their bodies.

❷ Now define the outline of the figure even more carefully. A line indicates the center back of the head, to show that it curves and turns a little. We look down to see a child, so the base of the T-shirt, the sleeves, and the shorts arc downward. However, on the back leg, which is lifting toward us, the lines arc upward.

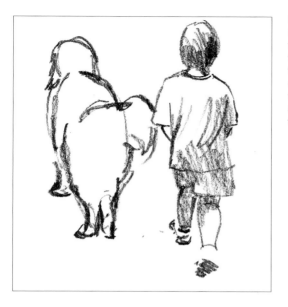

❸ Refine the shape of the dog and add some tone to the figure to show the light from above. Sketching the feet can be difficult, especially when a figure is walking or running, but just a few lines to hint at the feet may be enough.

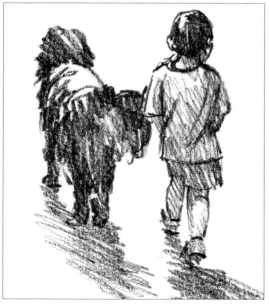

❹ Scribble is used for the shaggy dog, leaving a light area across its back to suggest its form. Add more shading to the boy, leaving light patches on the shoulder and the back calf; add shadows on the ground, then stop, or you'll overdo it.

want to know more?

Take it to the next level . . .

Go to . . .
► sketch a street scene—page 172
► walk on the beach in pastel pencils—page 182

Other sources
► **Photographs**
   useful sources of reference
► **Art galleries**
   look at portraits and pictures of animals
► **Sketchbooks**
   record your observations
► **Life drawing classes**
   find out if there are any in your area
► **Publications**
   visit www.harpercollins.com for HarperCollins
   art books

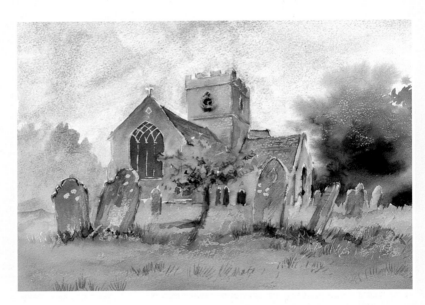

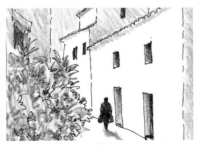

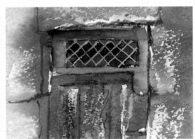

buildings

In order to draw a building accurately, you need an understanding of the rules of perspective and how to measure proportions. The good news is that once you have learned the simple basics of perspective and can measure accurately, you can solve any problems quickly and easily, and your sketches will have strength and authority.

Sketching buildings

Buildings, like people, need to be drawn accurately, otherwise
your sketch will look very weak. Sketching buildings means
tackling that supposedly frightening subject —perspective.
Perspective does not need to be terrifying, however, as long
as you take on board a few simple principles.

Basic rules

You learned how to measure proportions on page 70. When you are using
artists' measuring, do not forget to lock your elbow!

▶ Horizontal and vertical lines
in architecture are easy to
draw, as shown in this window.
You only need to be concerned
about the proportions.

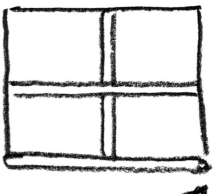

▼ When parallel lines (the top
and bottom of a window like
this, or a road or wall) recede
away from you, they create
angles. If you keep extending
these lines, they would meet
eventually at a "vanishing point."

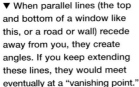

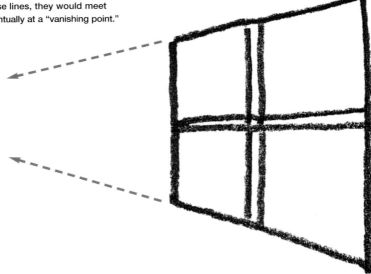

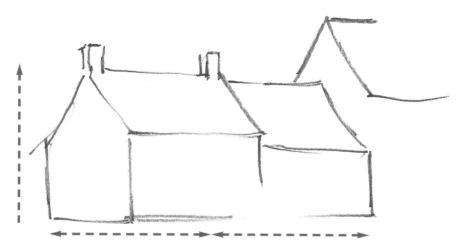

▲ First, draw what you see—then check the proportions. Never begin with the rules and then try to make the drawing fit; this is a common mistake. Draw freehand, trusting your eye. Then and only then, use the perspective "rules" to check your drawing's accuracy. Ensure that the proportions of your buildings are correct. Always start with the largest proportions and work down to the smaller ones, such as windows and doors. In this sketch the height of the buildings fits into the width twice.

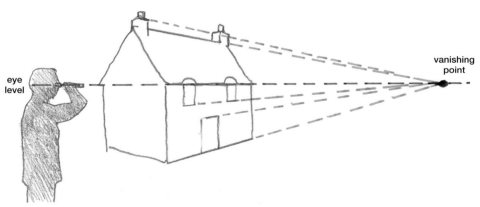

eye level

vanishing point

▲ Once the proportions are correct, you need to check any angles. To do this, you need to establish your eye level in the scene. Place your sketchbook on the bridge of your nose and then look across it at the scene. That will be your eye level. Now mark your eye level on your sketch. You must ensure that all the receding lines above your eye level travel down toward the eye level and that all the receding lines below your eye level travel up toward it. These lines should meet at a vanishing point, which sometimes can be off the paper or the sketchbook page.

Checking angles

Even if your angles meet neatly at a vanishing point, you may have misjudged them and made them too steep or too shallow. An excellent way to check this is with an angle gauge, which you can make from two pieces of cardboard held together with a clip.

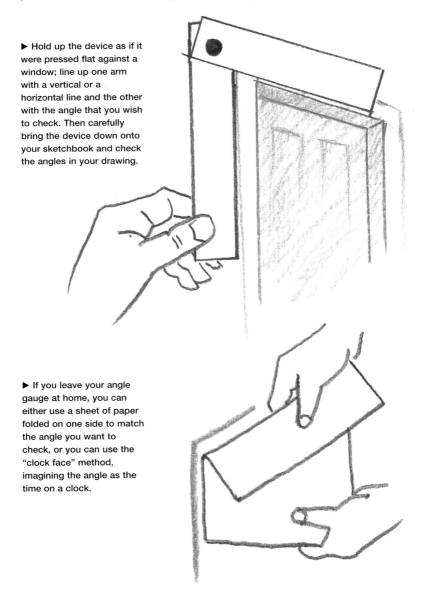

▶ Hold up the device as if it were pressed flat against a window; line up one arm with a vertical or a horizontal line and the other with the angle that you wish to check. Then carefully bring the device down onto your sketchbook and check the angles in your drawing.

▶ If you leave your angle gauge at home, you can either use a sheet of paper folded on one side to match the angle you want to check, or you can use the "clock face" method, imagining the angle as the time on a clock.

The shape of the sky

When you tackle a whole row of buildings or a street scene, it can be difficult to simplify the mass of buildings that you see and get the silhouette right. Try looking at the shape of the sky to help you.

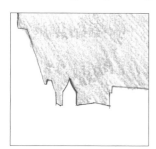

▲ "Seeing" the sky as a simple light shape against the rooftops is a helpful way to begin your sketch, instead of starting with the complexity of the buildings.

▶ When you are satisfied with the shape of the skyline, you can use the corners of the outline to drop down vertical lines, which will create the edges of the buildings. It is then much easier to position the doors and the windows.

MUST KNOW

Measuring
Without really accurate proportions, a building will not only look wrong or distorted, the windows and doors simply will not "fit." It is always a good idea to measure the largest proportions first— the height and width of a building—before dealing with the details.

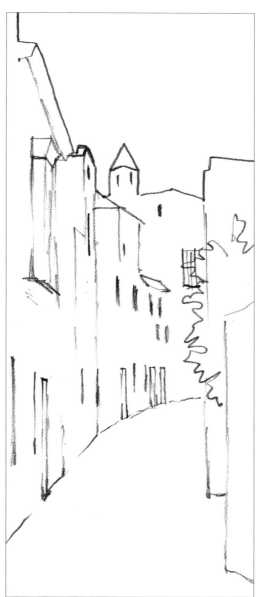

Windows and doorways

Look at the features of a building: doors and windows. You need to be accurate when you portray a window's construction and shape, but your painting can be looser and more interesting if you add details, like curtains.

❶ Draw in the main details. Apply masking fluid to the lace curtain details, and then you can start painting in the surrounding brickwork.

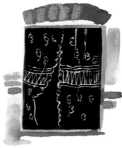
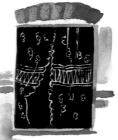

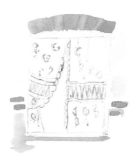

❷ Paint in the window area, using a mixture of brown and dark blue watercolor. Place in the bricks with some orange oil pastel.

Watercolors

Alizarin Crimson

Burnt Sienna

Indigo

Cadmium Orange

Yellow Ocher

Oil pastel

orange

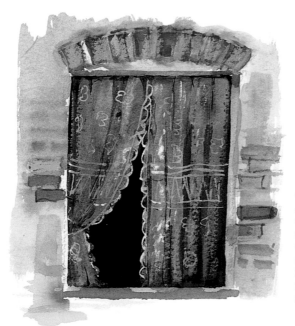

❸ Rub off the masking fluid. Apply up to three watery washes of white gouache over the curtains. Let each wash dry before applying the next one. Complete the brickwork using orange, red, and yellow watercolors and orange oil pastel.

Barn doorway

Another useful subject is a doorway, which, once you gain confidence, can be drawn to include people, animals, or plants in your future work.

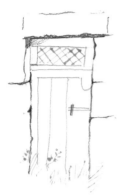

❶ Draw in the main features. With a brown watersoluble pencil, emphasize the door frame plus the start of the stonework. Apply masking fluid to the chicken wire at the top and to the grasses at the base of the door.

Watersoluble pencils

burnt sienna

dark brown

Oil pastels

cream

neutral gray

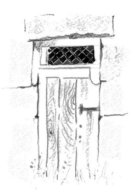

❷ Loosely apply cream and gray oil pastels to the stones and the door. Using burnt sienna watersoluble pencil, draw in the rusty hinge and the nail heads, plus the wood grain on the door. Paint dark gray over the top window section.

Watercolors

Neutral Gray

Cerulean

Olive Green

Payne's Gray

❸ Wash Neutral Gray watercolor across the stonework to emphasize the oil pastel work. Rub off the masking fluid and paint blue on the door and green over the grasses.

Roofs

Each section of a building has its own individual style, design, and materials. Look hard at the color, texture, and structure of some different roofs. It is amazing even just observing their colors, and the way in which the tiles fit into and jut up to each other. Try out several versions for yourself.

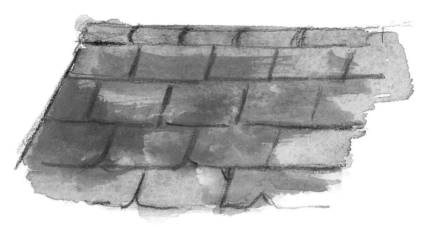

▲ This ordinary gray slate tile resembles brickwork. Each tile straddles the adjacent row, with a terra-cotta ridge capping the top.

▶ Pantiles are fabulous tiles that interlock to form ridges and patterns that are a joy to look at, but they are not easy to represent! Water-soluble sepia ink outlines these tiles, and violet and orange water-colors fill in the color of the roof.

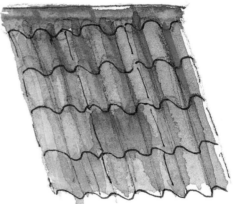

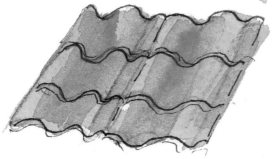

◀ One tile clips over another, forming an interesting flowing pattern. These are drawn in watersoluble inks with orange watercolors.

Brickwork

Studying the structure and texture of the material of any subject is essential, and brickwork is a good example of this. The colors vary considerably, and the weathering and aging of the bricks makes garden walls and paths more interesting. These examples have been painted on a sandy pastel paper.

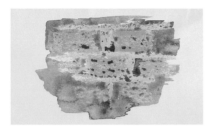

▲ Bricks and mortar are outlined in oil pastels, which act as a resist to the darker watercolors applied over the top.

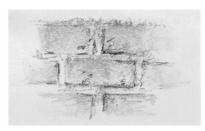

▲ Soft pastels are applied to the brick shapes and the mortar, and ink details added afterward.

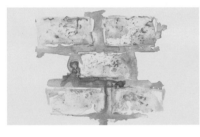

▲ Assorted watersoluble pencil shavings are splintered into the wet brick shapes to mingle. Gray watercolor mortar is added.

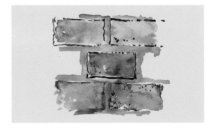

▲ Waterproof and watersoluble inks are then used for the brickwork, with gray watercolor used for the mortar.

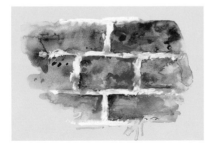

▲ Here, watercolors are applied wet-into-wet for the bricks, while white gouache is used to create the mortar.

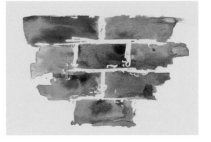

▲ Masking fluid is used for the mortar shapes, the bricks are added in watercolor then the masking fluid is rubbed off.

EXERCISE ## Sketch a street in pastel pencils

If you have lots of vacation photos in a drawer, see if you can find a simple street scene to sketch, like this Spanish one. Travel brochures are useful if you do not have any photographs. After using photos, try working from life.

The palette
Pastel pencils

red   orange   green   mauve   blue

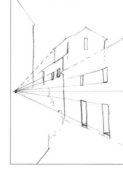

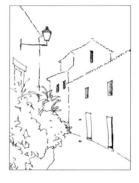

❶ Using pencil, lightly draw the main outlines of the street and the buildings. When working from life, always check the sky as well as the proportions of the roof shapes.

MUST KNOW

Adding figures
Placing a figure in a scene will always add interest to your work and will help to give it scale. The shadow it casts can provide a sense of sunshine.

❷ Drop down some vertical lines for the edges of the buildings and lightly draw a horizontal line for your eye level. Extend the lines of the rooftops on the right to meet at a vanishing point at eye level. Now position the windows and doors, checking to see where they are in relation to points on the roof and to each other. The angles of the tops and bottoms of the windows and doors will meet at the vanishing point.

❸ Switch to a black art pen or fine point pen. Draw the buildings using broken lines and suggest foliage on the left with scribble marks. When the pen marks are completely dry, erase the pencil construction lines. The two small dots to the left of the central doorway are there to show the position of a figure. This is a good tip—always make a note where a figure's head and feet lie in relation to the surroundings.

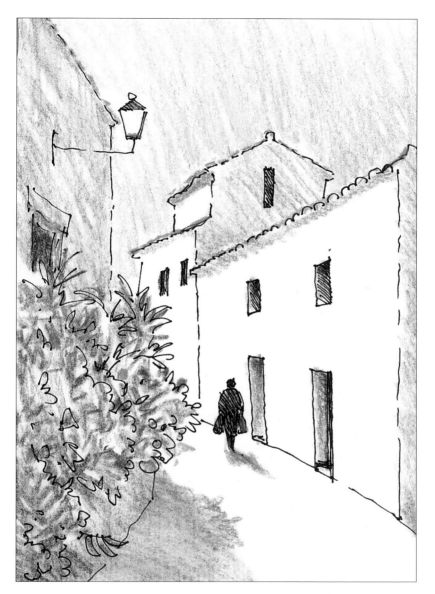

❹ Quickly add the figure—the less you
mess around with it, the better it will be. Do
not make the head too large. Use pastel
pencils and work over the pen drawing,
softening the color in places with your
fingers. The purple shadows will give a
wonderful feeling of strong Mediterranean
sunlight to your picture.

EXERCISE   Sketch a church in mixed media

A traditional church will provide you with an interesting and challenging subject. You can either work from photographs or quick sketches, or you may wish to take your art materials along with you and sketch in situ.

The palette

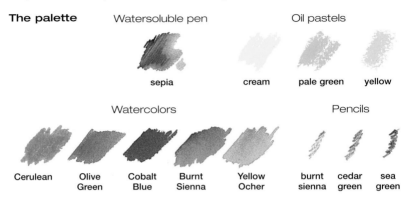

Watersoluble pen

sepia

Oil pastels

cream   pale green   yellow

Watercolors

Cerulean   Olive   Cobalt   Burnt   Yellow
            Green   Blue   Sienna   Ocher

Pencils

burnt   cedar   sea
sienna   green   green

❶ Sketch in all of the main details. Apply some masking fluid to the roof, the tops of the gravestones, grasses, church clock, and windows. Add dark areas with a sepia watersoluble art pen. Apply some yellow and pale green oil pastels to the grass areas.

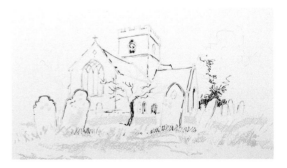

❷ Paint the sky Cerulean. Mix green and Cerulean for the trees, adding Cobalt Blue to the trees on the right with a little yellow at the top and on the front gravestones. Darken the windows and clock using Cobalt Blue; add brown plus yellow for the other gravestones. Paint the roof brown.

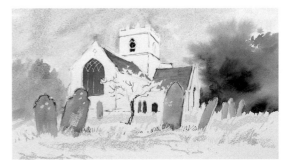

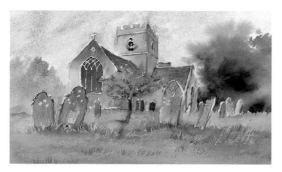

❸ When it is completely dry, paint in the middle distance using yellow and a touch of green. Then adding more Cerulean, paint in the foreground, then paint in the small tree details. Paint the church a mix of yellow, brown, and a little Cerulean.

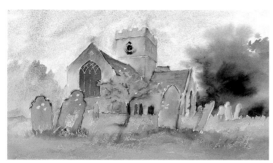

❹ When it has dried thoroughly, rub off the masking fluid, leaving the detailed white paper. Now gently merge the light areas into the background, brushing over it with yellow watercolor.

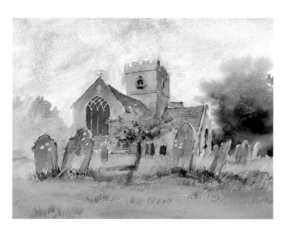

❺ Finished picture: white 140 lb (300 gsm) watercolor paper, 11 x 14 inches (28 x 36 cm). Using sea green pencil, detail in the final stages of the small tree in the foreground. Pencil in some foreground grasses using cedar green and burnt sienna. For extra light, gently apply the cream pastel over the distant tree surfaces, roof, and gravestones. Go over the undulating shadows connecting the front gravestones using Cobalt Blue with green watercolor.

want to know more?

Take it to the next level . . .

Go to . . .
▶ **composition**—page 36
▶ **foreground and distance**—page 40
▶ **sketching skies**—page 116

Other sources
▶ **Photographs**
   useful sources of reference
▶ **Sketchbooks**
   for keeping a record of what you see
▶ **Art exhibitions**
   visit or even show your own work
▶ **Local venues**
   may allow you to display/sell your work
▶ **Publications**
   visit www.harpercollins.com for
   HarperCollins art books

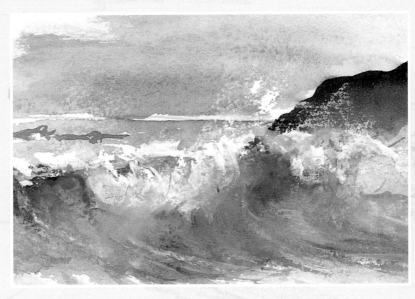

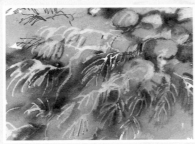

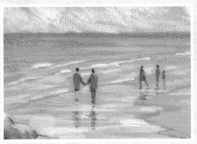

seaside

The seaside offers a richness and abundance of subjects for sketching. Your challenge is to convey the large expanse of open water, sky, and beach, with few trees or vegetation. The movement of the waves is different to inland water subjects. There are so many things to draw that you could keep a sketchbook just for seaside sketching.

▶ Seaside sketching

The seaside is a perfect place to sketch. There are so many possible subjects—sea, shore, boats, jetties, windbreaks— the list is endless, and in the limited space of a few pages, we can only hint at the variety of fascinating possibilities.

Sea

Let's begin with the sea. Sketching waves is fun, but it requires a high level of observation and concentration. Spend at least five minutes watching the way in which a wave rises and tumbles over, as well as how it changes color. When you begin to feel familiar with the pattern of movement, you can make a series of quick studies.

❶ Use horizontal strokes of bright blue watersoluble pencil for the horizon and the sea and curving strokes for the breaking waves. Block in the water behind the wave, leaving gaps for distant waves. Use a light yellow-green for the top and inside of the wave and blue for its shadow.

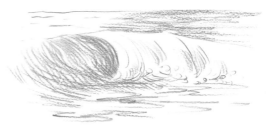

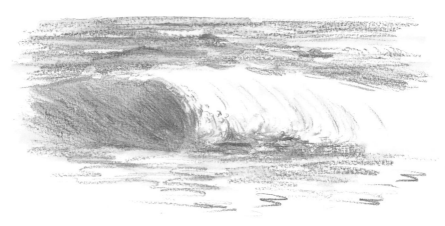

❷ With a wet brush, "loosen" the color. While the paper is wet, you can add more blue pencil if you have lifted too much color. When the paper is dry, use a craft knife to scratch the paper to create a few bubbles on the edge of the wave and for a few whitecaps.

bright blue   yellow-green

Rocks

Rocks on the beach will often have complex shapes, having been battered by the elements for a long time. By squinting, you can simplify their shapes into simple blocks. Always begin with the main, large shape and add details, such as cracks and textures, last.

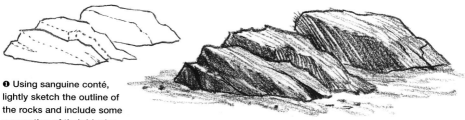

❶ Using sanguine conté, lightly sketch the outline of the rocks and include some suggestion of their blocky shapes, using a line to show where there is a change of plane. It helps to squint, to simplify the rock's shape.

❷ If light strikes the top of the rocks, then the side planes will receive less light. Use linear strokes of conté, building up a heavier concentration of strokes on the darker sides of the rocks, and add details, such as cracks.

Boats

Boats can be difficult to draw, since they bob around on the water, tilt on land, and have complicated curving shapes with bulges. Always accurately check the proportions, and study the shapes carefully. Choose simple shapes first and move on to boats with masts, rigging, and other paraphernalia.

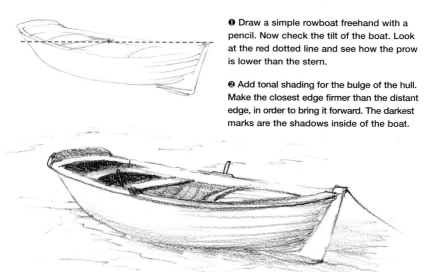

❶ Draw a simple rowboat freehand with a pencil. Now check the tilt of the boat. Look at the red dotted line and see how the prow is lower than the stern.

❷ Add tonal shading for the bulge of the hull. Make the closest edge firmer than the distant edge, in order to bring it forward. The darkest marks are the shadows inside of the boat.

Seaweed and pebbles

Pebbles are the sea's gorgeous jewelry, and seaweed is its underwater forest—a lucrative combination for the painter. When exposed at low tide, both are a testament to the variety and complexity of marine life. They offer an endless source of inspiration for mixing different media.

▶ This matted growth of bladder wrack, with their inflated oval fronds and bladders, are a familiar sight on rocks at the seashore in the summer. Olive Green, Burnt Sienna, and Cobalt Blue watercolors are painted with a narrow brush to show the weeds, rocks, stones, and distance. The stones in the foreground are splattered in with Sienna, and the highlights on the seaweed are dotted in using cream oil pastel.

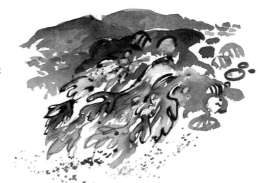

▼ This red, feathered seaweed is common in rock pools at low tide and clings to shells and stones. Masking fluid and sepia watersoluble ink are used for the initial details. More details are then added with a waterproof sepia art pen. After wetting the whole drawing with water and letting it dry, the masking fluid is rubbed off, and a watercolor wash of light Yellow Ocher is painted over to unite the whole picture.

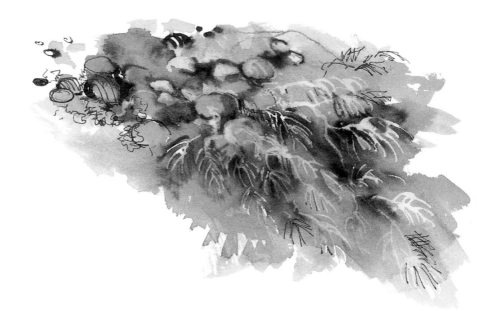

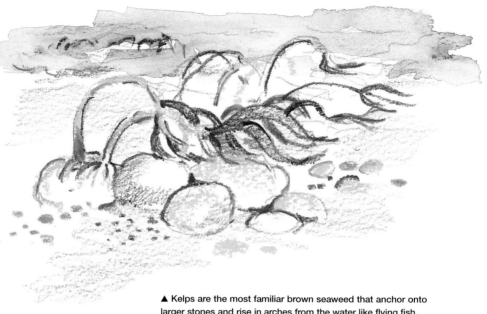

▲ Kelps are the most familiar brown seaweed that anchor onto larger stones and rise in arches from the water like flying fish. Yellow ocher, burnt sienna, and sepia watersoluble pencils are used with gray oil pastels for the stone texturing. Everything is kept dry, except for the cobalt blue added from the tip of a watersoluble pencil with a brush for the distant sea.

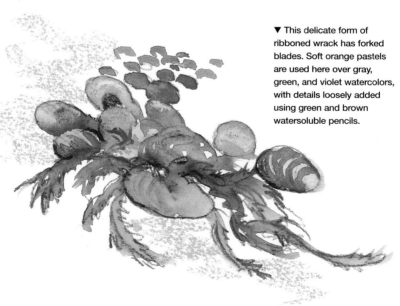

▼ This delicate form of ribboned wrack has forked blades. Soft orange pastels are used here over gray, green, and violet watercolors, with details loosely added using green and brown watersoluble pencils.

EXERCISE | ## Walk on the beach in pastel pencils

Putting a few figures into a scene will immediately add a sense of scale. The figures in this sketch are only suggested, but their small size helps emphasize the vast expanse of the ocean and the beach.

The palette

Pastel pencils | Art pen

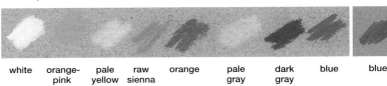

| white | orange-pink | pale yellow | raw sienna | orange | pale gray | dark gray | blue | blue |

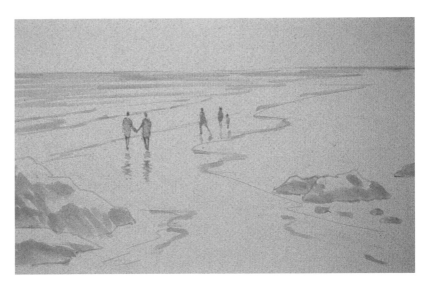

❶ On blue-gray pastel paper draw the scene with an art pen. Use the brush tip to block in the darker sides of the rocks and add horizontal strokes for the sea. The people's heads are all in line (except for the child). Try to get their proportions right.

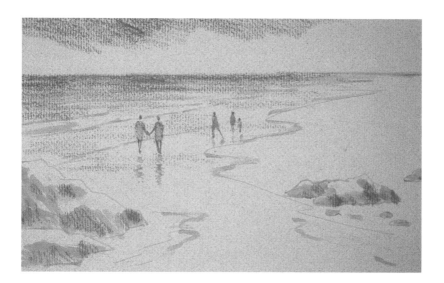

❷ Switch to pastel pencils and scribble in some blue for the sky and some horizontal strokes for the sea. Also, put some blue onto the darker sides of the rocks. We are going to build up the rocks with lots of different colors to make them interesting.

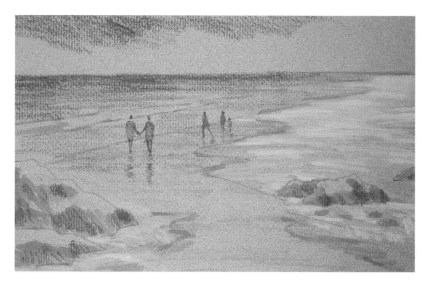

❸ Use yellow and raw sienna for the sand. Wet sand is darker than dry sand. In the foreground separate your strokes a little to suggest undulations in the surface. In the distance use sweeping, horizontal strokes that blend together naturally.

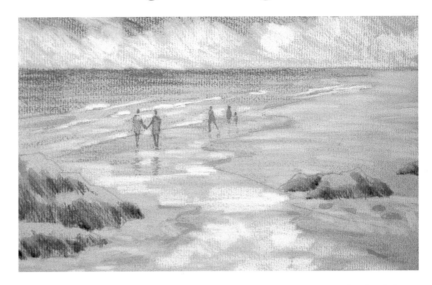

❹ Use white for the clouds, edge the waves, and the water on the sand, pressing hard where the clouds are reflected. Change the direction of your strokes in the clouds for a lively effect. Use dark gray and a little raw sienna on the darker sides of the rocks.

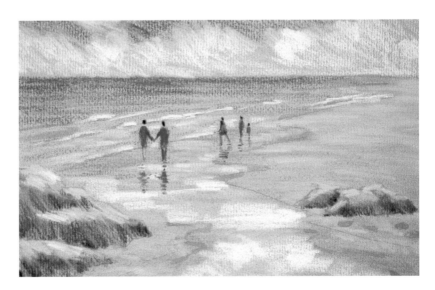

❺ Tiny strokes of color can indicate the people's clothes, and you can use the same colors with some small, horizontal, broken strokes for the reflections. Use dark gray for the heads. Work more detail into the rocks with some pale gray.

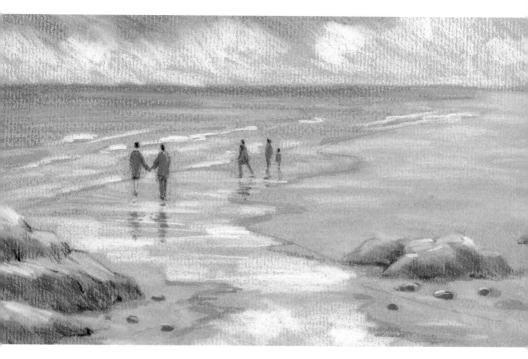

❺ Finished picture: Pastel paper, 6 x 9 inches (15 x 23 cm). Add a few dark gray pebbles, with a touch of a lighter color on the top. Stroke a little blue at the base of the rocks for the shadows. You can suggest a few cracks in the rocks with some dark gray, and add a few strokes of orange-pink to the sand. Finally, you can help slightly break up the people's reflections just by using a few horizontal strokes.

MUST KNOW

Check the horizon

When you are sketching, you should always check to make sure that the horizon is, in fact, horizontal and perfectly parallel with the top of your paper. So many beginners' drawings are spoiled by horizons that slope upward or downward. If you are uncertain, check your horizon with a set square.

A seascape in watercolor

A lasting memory of the seaside is the tumbling and unfurling waves. Each wave unravels and splashes against rocks and along the shore. This exercise tries to capture this movement and bring the sea to life.

❶ Using a 2B pencil, lightly and roughly sketch in the main elements of the waves and the rocks.

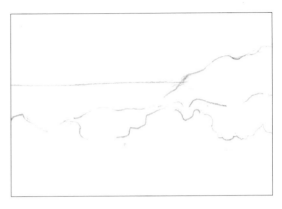

❷ Mix a brown with Raw Umber and a little Cerulean watercolor, and paint in the mid-distance rocks, making the edges slightly misty where the top of the waves will come. Paint in the underside of the wave with Cerulean.

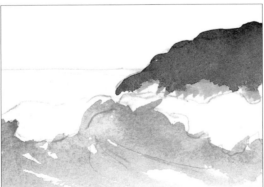

❸ Use Cobalt Blue for the distant expanse of sea to contrast with the foreground wave. Paint Neutral Gray into the sky shape, grading it so that it is darker toward the sea, and then blending it with a little Cerulean on the left.

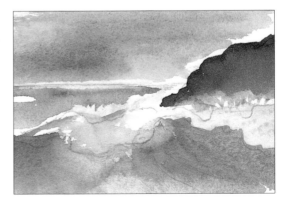

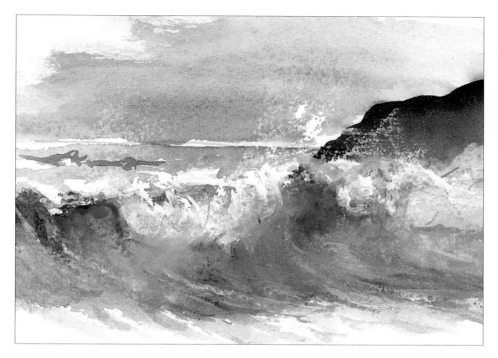

❹ Darken the underside of the waves with an additional wash of Cerulean and Cobalt Blue. When it is dry, splatter watery white gouache against the wave edges for the spray. Add small, directional lines of Cobalt Blue to the foreground wave to complete the picture.

The palette
Watercolor

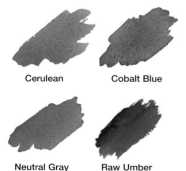

Cerulean   Cobalt Blue

Neutral Gray   Raw Umber

want to know more?

Take it to the next level . . .

Go to . . .
▶ **watercolor techniques**—page 31
▶ **sketching water**—page 128
▶ **moving water**—page 130

Other sources
▶ **Photographs**
  useful sources of reference
▶ **Art shows**
  look out for local or national events
▶ **Internet**
  interactive CD-ROMs
▶ **Painting vacations**
  expand your horizons with other artists
▶ **Publications**
  visit www.harpercollins.com for HarperCollins art books

Need to know more?

There is a wealth of further information that is available to artists, especially if you have access to the Internet. Listed below are just some of the organizations, magazines, art shows and societies, book clubs, and Internet resources that you might find useful to help you develop your drawing and sketching and experiment with working in other media.

Museums

Smithsonian American Art Museum
www.americanart.si.edu

Smithsonian National Portrait Gallery
www.npg.si.edu

Metropolitan Museum of Art
1000 Fifth Avenue
New York, New York 10028
www.metmuseum.org

Art Magazines

The Artist's Magazine
4700 E. Galbraith Rd.
Cincinnati, OH 45236
www.artistsmagazine.com

American Artist
770 Broadway
New York, NY 10003
www.myamericanartist.com

International Artist
International Artist Publishing
PO Box 469068
Escondido, CA 92046
www.internationalartist.com

Art Supplies

Daler-Rowney USA
2 Corporate Drive
Cranbury, New Jersey 08512
www.daler-rowney.com

Faber-Castell USA, Inc.
9450 Allen Drive
Cleveland, Ohio 44125
www.faber-castellusa.com

Mohawk Paper Mills, Inc
PO Box 497
Cohoes, New York 12047
www.mohawkpaper.com

Pentel of America
Corporate Headquarters
2805 Columbia Street
Torrance, CA 90509
www.pentel.com

Art Societies

The Society of Illustrators
Museum of American Illustration at the
Society of Illustrators
128 East 63rd Street
New York, NY 10021
www.societyillustrators.org

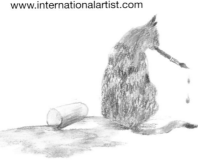

Online Resources

Art Museum Network
The official website of the world's
leading art museums
www.amn.org

The Artlist
Extensive listings of art shows,
juried competitions, and
contests etc.
www.theartlist.com

ArtShow
Listings of shows, workshops,
and resources
www.artshow.com

Painters Online
Interactive art club run by The
Artist's Publishing Company
www.painters-online.com

WetCanvas
This is part magazine, part virtual
classroom, and part reference site. It is the
largest community site on the internet with
a specific focus on the practising visual
artist. It concentrates on providing the
following services to visitors and members:
● A virtual community where artists can
share ideas, critiques, and other
information
● Tools for managing and promoting
virtual/online galleries of work
● A complete array of art lessons and
tutorials for all levels of artists
● Product comparison and research
information for art supplies and services
● An image library
www.wetcanvas.com

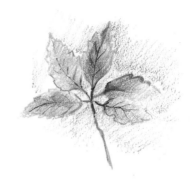

Index

Numerals in italics refer to illustrations

angles, checking 166, *166*
animals 156–161
apple 61, *61*, 62
art brush pens 15, 30, *140–141*

banana 55, *55*
bark 76, *76*, 103, *103*
blended edges 31, *31*
blocking in 31, *31*
boats 179, *179*
brickwork 171, *171*
brushes 17
buildings 164–175, *164–175*
bulldog clips 17

charcoal sticks 15, 21, *21*, *117*, *122–123*, *128*
cherry 60, *60*
church 174–175, *174–175*
circles 44, *44*
clouds 116–125, *116–125*
colored inks 16
colored pencils 15, *56*, *132–133*
colored wax pencils 27, *27*
colors 40
composition 36–39
compressed charcoal 15
cones 43, *43*
conté 15, 22, *22*, *112–113*, *122–123*, *154–155*
cool colors 40
corners 39
counterchange 38, *38*
cows 156, *156*
craft knives 17
cygnets 158–159, *158–159*
cylinders 42, *42*

daisies 92–93, *92–93*
dandelions 96, *96*, 97, *97*
depth 40, 139, *139*
distance 40–41, 138, 144–145

dog 160–161
doorways 168–169, *168–169*
drawing board 17
drawing pens 16

easel 17
edges 49, *49*
erasers 17

feathers 75, *75*
felt-tip pens 16, 30
fiber-tip pens 16, 30
figures 152–155, *152–155*, 172
fixative 17, 19, 21
flowers 86–87, 90–99
focal point 37, 39
foreground 40–41, 140–141
form 46–47, *46–47*
fruits 54–67

graded color washes 31, *31*
graphite lead pencils 20, *20*

horizon 185

inks 16

kitten 157, *157*

lakes 132–133
landscapes 138–149
lead pencils 15, 20
leaves 88–89, *88–89*, 105, *105*, 106, *106*
light 42–45
lifting out 31, *31*
lilac 87, *87*

marker pens 30
masking fluid 17, 32, *32*
materials 14–19
measuring proportions 70, 164, 167
melon 63, *63*
middle distance 142–143
mixed media 33, *33*, *57*, 66–67, *66–67*, *142–143*, *174–175*
mushroom 70, *70*

nectarine 55, *55*

oil pastels 6, 26, *26*, 96
onion 68–69, *68–69*
orange 58, *58*

palettes 17
paper 18, 19
pastel pencils 15, 23, *23*, *98–99*, *146–149*, *172–173*, *182–185*
pastels 16, 24–25, *24–25*, 92–95, *120–121*, *124–125*, *134–135*
on colored paper 26, *26*, 93, *144–145*, *158–159*
patterns 74–79
pear 54, *54*
pebbles 74, *74*, 180
pens 16, 30, *30*
people 152–155, *152–155*, 160–161, *160–161*
pepper 71, *71*
plants 86–99
plums 59, *59*
poppies 94–95, *94–95*, 97
proportions, measuring 70, 164, 167
pyramids 43, *43*

reflections 129, *129*
rocks 179, *179*
roofs 170, *170*

salts 32, *32*, 110
sea 178, *178*, 182–185, 186–187
seaside 178–187, *178–187*
seaweed 180–181, *180–181*
seedpod 77, *77*
shading 42–45
shadows 47–48, *47–48*, 140
shapes 42–45, *45*, 74–79
sheep 156, *156*
shells 78–83, *78–83*
sketchbooks 18
skies 116–125, 167
soft edges 31, *31*
spheres 44, *44*
squares 42, *42*
still life 64–65, *64–65*
strawberries 56, *56*, 57

street scene 172–173,
  172–173
swans 158–159, *158–159*

three-dimensional
  objects 46–49
torchons 17
trees 76, 102–113
  seasonal 107–109
triangles 43, *43*
tulips 91, *91*
vanishing point 164, *164,*

165, *165*, 166
vegetables 68–71
viewfinder, making a 36,
  36

warm colors 40
washes 31, *31*
water 128–135
waterfall 131, *131,*
  134–135, *134–135*
watercolors 17, 31, *31,*
  95, 96, 110–111, 168,

169, 186–187
watersoluble colored
  pencils 15, 28–29,
  28–29, 118–119, 169
waves 130, *130,* 178,
  178
wax pencils, colored 27,
  27, 80–83
wet-into-wet technique
  31, *31*
white gouache 17
windows 168, *168*

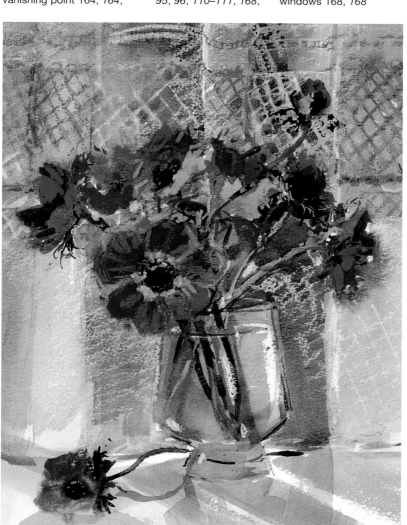